101 Top Secret Techniques Used by Successful Part Time Weekend Art Dealers

by David Valin

Copyright ©2016

For information on book distributions, or translations, please contact Antoine Versailles Publishing at:

info@antoineversaillespublishing.com

ISBN 13 978-1-884939-74-7

Published by Antoine Versailles Publishing

Cover Design and Photography by Yonja Valin

101 Top Secret Techniques Used by Successful Part Time Weekend Art Dealers

101 Top Secret Techniques Used by Successful Part Time Weekend Art Dealers is a book that shows you step by step techniques for you to become a part time weekend art dealer. It is a very good tool, for the person that wants to learn about art, and art dealing, and wants to get into being an art dealer without spending a lot of time or money.

There are many opportunities out in the current world for potential art enthusiasts, collectors, and marketers to benefit from. And weekend art dealing is a fun, adventurous and exciting thing to do.

The book encourages, learning about art, and artists, and also encourages the promotion and discovery of new as well as established artists and artworks. The book also has many sales prices of art, references to great art research libraries, and places to sell your art. The book also has included many successful techniques that have been used by the author for many years, and by many part time art dealers the author has met in his travels.

a grateful and humble author...

I created this book mainly for me to be able to communicate my journey to people, so that they can learn from my knowledge that I experienced in the world of art dealing. The perspective I give can help anyone run a successful business. Today in our ever changing world we have too many mono culture corporate careers. So I wrote this book to be a good guide, useful through good or bad economic times, mainly for the independent small business regular person that is interested in art and the creative exciting world of artists.

In this book I also am trying to motivate young people to get involved in the business of art, and have tried to emphasize in this book how important this is to the world. I think all people should create art, and that there should be people out there promoting the sales and purchasing of these peoples expressions of their creativity. What if art was appreciated, by all people, and the problems of the world were decided by creatively happy people? Don't You Think that the world would be a greater place, with less greed based ideas?

So without further ideal thinking I wish you all the best in your Art related ventures, and know you will find a treasure, or promote a young or old artist and You will be better off for the journey...   --David Valin

Table of Contents

TOP SECRET TECHNIQUE 1 YOU CAN BE A SUCCESSFUL ART DEALER FOR LITTLE OR NO MONEY..........................17

TOP SECRET TECHNIQUE 2 HOW TO SET UP YOUR ART DEALER REFERENCE DESK, LIBRARY AND ART GALLERY IN YOUR HOME..........................19

TOP SECRET TECHNIQUE 3 OLD ART IS NOT ALWAYS THE ONLY ART THAT HAS A VALUE..........................21

TOP SECRET TECHNIQUE 4 ARTISTS MULTIPLE PRINTS HAVE A GREAT VALUE AND RESALE VALUE ALSO..........23

EXAMPLE PRINT AUCTION RECORD SALES:..................24

TOP SECRET TECHNIQUE 5 ARE YOU CRAZY? YOU CAN'T MAKE MONEY DOING THAT!..........................27

TOP SECRET TECHNIQUE 6 THE BABY BOOMER ART GOLD RUSH!..........................29

TOP SECRET TECHNIQUE 7 ART CAN BE FOUND EVERYWHERE..........................31

TOP SECRET TECHNIQUE 8 BUY ANY ABSTRACT WORKS OF ART DATED BETWEEN 1900 AND 1950..........................33

TOP SECRET TECHNIQUE 9 OLD MASTER PAINTINGS CAN STILL BE DISCOVERED AND ACQUIRED TODAY!....35

TOP SECRET TECHNIQUE 10 HOW MUCH SHOULD YOU OFFER FOR ART AT OUTSIDE SALES?..........................36

TOP SECRET TECHNIQUE 11 HOW DO YOU TELL THE DIFFERENCE BETWEEN PRINTS AND DRAWINGS, AND ORIGINAL ART?..39

TOP SECRET TECHNIQUE 12 VIDEO AND DIGITAL CAMERA RESEARCH TIPS..43

TOP SECRET TECHNIQUE 12B THE DIGITAL CAMERA IS ALSO A GREAT TOOL FOR THE ART RESEARCH PERSON 45

TOP SECRET TECHNIQUE 13 PICK UP USED AUCTION AND GALLERY CATALOGS..47

TOP SECRET TECHNIQUE 14 PICK UP USED ART MAGAZINES..49

TOP SECRET TECHNIQUE 15 SPEND SOME TIME IN ART MUSEUMS..51

TOP SECRET TECHNIQUE 16 GO TO ART GALLERY SHOWS..53

TOP SECRET TECHNIQUE 17 LOOK FOR ART AUCTION LABELS, AND GALLERY LABELS..55

HERE ARE SOME POPULAR ART AUCTION HOUSES:......55

TOP SECRET TECHNIQUE 18 LABELS ON AN ARTWORK CAN TELL YOU NOTHING OR EVERYTHING ABOUT THE ARTWORK!..57

MUSEUM, EXHIBITION OR GALLERY LABELS CAN MEAN ONE OF 4 THINGS..58

TOP SECRET TECHNIQUE 19 HOW TO TELL IF A WORK OF ART IS THE AGE IT LOOKS...............................59

THREE STEPS TO IDENTIFICATION....................................61

TOP SECRET TECHNIQUE 20 ASK PEOPLE AND LOOK FOR ANY OLD PAINTINGS EVEN, TORN PAINTINGS!.......63

TOP SECRET TECHNIQUE 21 ALWAYS HAVE AT LEAST $100 CASH ON YOU TO SPEND AT SALES........................65

TOP SECRET TECHNIQUE 22 THREE IMPORTANT WORDS, RESEARCH, RESEARCH, RESEARCH!...............67

TOP SECRET TECHNIQUE 23 GET TO KNOW YOUR ART DEALER COMPETITION...69

TOP SECRET TECHNIQUE 24 HOW TO GET THE MOST CASH FOR YOUR ART...71

TOP SECRET TECHNIQUE 25 SHOW YOUR ART TO SEVERAL PEOPLE AND CREATE DIALOGUE....................77

TOP SECRET TECHNIQUE 26 HAVE DINNERS FOR POTENTIAL ART CUSTOMERS..79

TOP SECRET TECHNIQUE 27 GET TO KNOW AN ART CONSERVATOR OR RESTORER...80

TOP SECRET TECHNIQUE 28 LITTLE KNOWN TOP SECRET, BE A SELF MADE EXPERT PHD IN IDENTIFYING FRAMES...83

TOP SECRET TECHNIQUE 29 IF IT WALKS LIKE A DUCK, AND TALKS LIKE A DUCK IT MIGHT BE A DUCK OR FORGERY OF A DUCK!.....................86

TOP SECRET TECHNIQUE 30 TOP SECRET ART DEALER TOOL THE CATALOG RAISONNE.........................87

TOP SECRET TECHNIQUE 31 EVERY TIME YOU PLACE A WORK OF ART YOU MIGHT BE MAKING HISTORY!..........89

TOP SECRET TECHNIQUE 32 PLACES FOR ART DISCOVERY.................................91

TOP SECRET TECHNIQUE 33 TECHNIQUES USED FOR LOOKING AT THE PRICING STRUCTURE OF ART FROM THE NEAR PAST TO THE PRESENT.......................95

TOP SECRET TECHNIQUE 34 FIND AT LEAST ONE WORK OF ART EVERY WEEK THAT YOU KNOW YOU CAN SELL 99

TOP SECRET TECHNIQUE 35 THE YARD SALE "AUCTION", AND HOW TO PREVENT IT.................................101

TOP SECRET TECHNIQUE 36 RESEARCHING THE ARTIST FOR CLUES ABOUT ART.................................103

TOP SECRET TECHNIQUE 37 DECORATE WITH INVESTMENT GRADE FINE ART WORKS.........................105

TOP SECRET TECHNIQUE 38 COLLECTING IS INEVITABLE WITH THE TRUE ART DEALER!.....................107

TOP SECRET TECHNIQUE 39 LETTERS AT AN ARTIST ESTATE CAN BE ENLIGHTENING TREASURES!...............109

TOP SECRET TECHNIQUE 40 HOW TO TELL THE DATE OF A WORK OF ART..111

TOP SECRET TECHNIQUE 41 ART RESEARCH ON WORKS ON PAPER IS LIKE SHERLOCK HOLMES, SIMPLE DEDUCTION WATSON!..113

TOP SECRET TECHNIQUE 42 YOU CAN MAKE $1000 OR EVEN $100,000 EXTRA CASH, AS A PART TIME ART DEALER!..115

TOP SECRET TECHNIQUE 43 THE GYPSY HARVEST BALL EVERY OCTOBER!...117

TOP SECRET TECHNIQUE 44 FLASHLIGHT PEOPLE IN MINK COATS!...119

TOP SECRET TECHNIQUE 45 HOW TO DISPLAY ART FOR MAXIMUM PROFITS!...123

TOP SECRET TECHNIQUE 46 ATTEND OFTEN, EVERY MONTH LOCAL ANTIQUE AUCTIONS!...............................125

TOP SECRET TECHNIQUE 47 BLIND FOLD ME, TAKE ME TO ANY TOWN, AND I WILL FIND A VALUABLE WORK OF ART IN A SHORT TIME OVER THE WEEKEND!.................127

TOP SECRET TECHNIQUE 48 HOW TO SET UP YOUR ART DEALER NETWORK..129

TOP SECRET TECHNIQUE 49 BE AWARE OF OTHER TREASURES BESIDES ART..131

TOP SECRET TECHNIQUE 51 AUCTION ESTIMATES AND REALITY OF PRICE...133

TOP SECRET TECHNIQUE 52 REGIONAL ART TREASURE HUNTING...135

TOP SECRET TECHNIQUE 53 ALWAYS TAKE AN ARTIST PRICE GUIDE WITH YOU ON YOUR WEEKEND ART EXCURSIONS!...137

TOP SECRET TECHNIQUE 54 ECONOMY GETS WORSE THEN, MORE ART GETS DISCOVERED!.........................139

TOP SECRET TECHNIQUE 55 THE DIFFERENT LEVELS OF BEING AN ART DEALER...141

TOP SECRET TECHNIQUE 56 THE BEST IN ART ALWAYS SEEMS TO HOLD ITS VALUE..143

TOP SECRET TECHNIQUE 57 LEARN HOW TO SPEAK IN ART DEALER LANGUAGE...147

TOP SECRET TECHNIQUE 58 HOW TO MANAGE, YOUR ART INVENTORY WISELY...149

TOP SECRET TECHNIQUE 59 JAPANESE WOODBLOCK BONANZA...151

TOP SECRET TECHNIQUE 60 THE DIFFERENT MEDIUMS ART IS CREATED IN MATERIALS AND TECHNIQUES OF ARTWORKS...153

TOP SECRET TECHNIQUE 61 HOW TO VIEW AN ARTWORK FOR MAXIMUM DISCOVERY.........................159

TOP SECRET TECHNIQUE 62 ART DEALING IS SOMETHING LIKE A TRUMPET. IF YOU DON'T PUT ANYTHING IN, YOU WON'T GET ANYTHING OUT...........161

TOP SECRET TECHNIQUE 63 WHEN BUYING ART DON'T WORRY ABOUT FAILURE. WORRY ABOUT THE CHANCES YOU MISS WHEN YOU DON'T EVEN TRY.........................163

TOP SECRET TECHNIQUE 64 EVERY GREAT ACHIEVEMENT WAS ONCE IMPOSSIBLE UNTIL AN INDIVIDUAL SET A GOAL TO MAKE IT A REALITY...........165

TOP SECRET TECHNIQUE 65 SCHEDULE INDEPENDENT ART RESEARCH TIME AND FREE TIME..........................167

TOP SECRET TECHNIQUE 66 BUILD A SUPPORTIVE COMMUNITY AND NURTURE IT, EVERY DAY..................169

TOP SECRET TECHNIQUE 67 MANAGE YOUR THOUGHTS, AND THE WAY YOU LOOK AT AN ARTWORK 171

TOP SECRET TECHNIQUE 68 LIFE IS A DARING ADVENTURE, IN ART DEALING OR NOTHING.................173

TOP SECRET TECHNIQUE 69 PUT YOUR MONEY WHERE IT WILL REAP THE MOST REWARDS..............................175

TOP SECRET TECHNIQUE 70 IS IT THE RIGHT TIME TO SELL THAT WORK OF ART?..177

TOP SECRET TECHNIQUE 71 CONTROL THE CASH THAT YOU USE, TO SPEND ON ART!...179

TOP SECRET TECHNIQUE 72 DEDICATE AT LEAST TWO HOURS A WEEK TO, MARKETING YOUR ART.................181

TOP SECRET TECHNIQUE 73 EQUALIZE YOUR SALES OF ART AND PROFIT GOALS..183

TOP SECRET TECHNIQUE 74 EVERY DOLLAR IN ART EXPENSE SHOULD BE DIRECTLY TIED TO GREATER CASH INCOME FORMULA.....................................187

TOP SECRET TECHNIQUE 75 THE ULTIMATE PROFITABLE WEEKEND ART DEALER MICRO BUSINESS...................191

TOP SECRET TECHNIQUE 76 DO NOT EVEN THINK ABOUT LEAVING FUN OUT OF THE FORMULA FOR SUCCESS IN YOUR WEEKEND ART BUSINESS..............193

TOP SECRET TECHNIQUE 77 MASTER YOUR ART RESEARCH AND REFERENCE TOOLS, INCLUDING THE WAY YOU THINK...195

TOP SECRET TECHNIQUE 78 BE PASSIONATE WITH YOUR ART RESEARCH AND DEALING............................197

TOP SECRET TECHNIQUE 79 FOCUS ON YOUR STRENGTHS...199

TOP SECRET TECHNIQUE 80 NEVER CONSIDER THE POSSIBILITY OF FAILURE IN, YOUR ART RESEARCH....201

TOP SECRET TECHNIQUE 81 LOOK FOR WAYS TO NETWORK IN THE ART WORLD.....................................203

TOP SECRET TECHNIQUE 82 USE THE INTERNET OFTEN FOR ART INFORMATION...207

TOP SECRET TECHNIQUE 83 YOU DO NOT NEED TO BE A PHD GRADUATE TO SUCCEED IN YOUR OWN ART BUSINESS...209

TOP SECRET TECHNIQUE 84 TO SUCCEED, IN ART DEALING YOU MUST BE WILLING TO ASK QUESTIONS, REMAIN CURIOUS, AND OPEN TO NEW KNOWLEDGE..211

TOP SECRET TECHNIQUE 85 LIKE A SAMURAI IN THE BEGINNING, YOU MIGHT FALL DOWN 7 TIMES, BUT GET UP 8!..213

TOP SECRET TECHNIQUE 86 ANYONE CAN DO THIS, YOU ARE THE PRODUCT OF YOUR OWN CHOOSING...214

TOP SECRET TECHNIQUE 87 ADVENTURE IS THERE, WAITING FOR YOU EVERY WEEKEND............................215

TOP SECRET TECHNIQUE 88 MAKING A PROFIT, NOT A LIVING IN YOUR ART DEALER BUSINESS......................216

TOP SECRET TECHNIQUE 89 LEARN FROM THE MISTAKES OF OTHERS, AND SOMETIMES YOURS!.......217

TOP SECRET TECHNIQUE 90 KNOWING THE WHO, WHAT, WHERE AND WHY OF THE AVERAGE ART CUSTOMER.218

TOP SECRET TECHNIQUE 91 NEVER LOSE SIGHT OF YOUR END GOAL OR YOUR DREAM OF ART TREASURE 220

TOP SECRET TECHNIQUE 92 IF IT WERE EASY TO FIND A PICASSO, EVERYBODY WOULD BE RICH! BUT, IT HAPPENS, MORE THAN YOU THINK!................................221

TOP SECRET TECHNIQUE 93 ARE YOU CRAZY? YOU CAN'T MAKE MONEY DOING THAT!................................222

TOP SECRET TECHNIQUE 94 SURVIVAL IN THE WEEKEND ART DEALER WORLD IS DEPENDENT UPON YOUR PERSEVERANCE...223

TOP SECRET TECHNIQUE 95 DECIDE NOW THAT YOU CAN START AN ART BUSINESS THAT YOU'LL ENJOY!...224

TOP SECRET TECHNIQUE 96 GETTING MARRIED TO AN ART RESEARCH PROJECT AND STICKING, WITH IT TOO LONG...225

TOP SECRET TECHNIQUE 97 THE SECRET, OF MAKING MONEY, WITH YOUR SMALL BUSINESS IS SIMPLE!.......227

TOP SECRET TECHNIQUE 98 SHOW IT OFF TO YOUR NETWORK!..229

TOP SECRET TECHNIQUE 99 SET REALISTIC GOALS FOR YOUR ART ADVENTURES.......................................231

TOP SECRET TECHNIQUE 100 TRAPS AND MISTAKES TO AVOID!..233

TOP SECRET TECHNIQUE 101 STRATEGIES AND TECHNIQUES TO HELP YOU IN BAD ECONOMIC TIMES!
....235

TOP SECRET TECHNIQUE 102 DO NOT THINK A MILLION-DOLLAR PAINTING WILL NOT BE DISCOVERED FOR $50 ON EBAY, EBID OR OTHER ONLINE AUCTIONS!.............237

TOP SECRET TECHNIQUE 103 TAKE AN ASPIRING ARTIST WHOSE WORK YOU ADMIRE TO DINNER!.......................239

TOP SECRET TECHNIQUE 104 HOW TO SET UP YOUR WEEKEND PART TIME ART DEALER'S ART GALLERY IN YOUR HOME!..241

TOP SECRET TECHNIQUE 105 THE MUSEUM CURATOR CAN SOMETIMES BE YOUR BEST FRIEND!....................245

TOP SECRET TECHNIQUE 106 ALWAYS REMEMBER... THERE ARE 4 REASONS SUCCESSFUL ART DEALERS DO WHAT THEY DO..247

TOP SECRET TECHNIQUE 107 ART DISCOVERIES WILL BE HERE FOR A WHILE..249

TOP SECRET TECHNIQUE 108 THE GOOD ART GALLERY OR THE BAD ART GALLERY..251

TOP SECRET TECHNIQUE 109 ART PRICES ARE LIKE STOCK PRICES THEY, GO UP AND THEY GO DOWN.....255

TOP SECRET TECHNIQUE 110 SOCIALIZE WITH ARTISTS 257

TOP SECRET TECHNIQUE 111 ART IS A CONVERSATION CREATOR...259

ART GALLERIES THAT BUY AND SELL WORKS OF ART 261

TOP SECRET TECHNIQUE 112 LEARN ALL THE STYLES OF ART..269

POP ART...269

OTHER PERIODS OF ART STYLES WITH ARTISTS OF THAT PERIOD..314

SOME OTHER GREAT ART REFERENCE AND ART DEALER MAGAZINES YOU SHOULD BE ON THE LOOKOUT FOR..391

SOME EXAMPLES OF ANTIQUE FRAME AUCTION SALES RECORDS..395

PLACES ART DEALERS BUY, SELL AND AUCTION ART. 396

SPECIAL ART DEALER RESEARCH LIBRARIES.............402

BIBLIOGRAPHY..408

ABOUT THE AUTHOR...
....416

Top Secret Technique 1 You can be a successful art dealer for little or no money

Yes, anyone can be an art dealer for little or no money investment. This sounds a little strange, that an art dealer business requires very little money to run, but it is true. Some art dealers will earn $3000 to $5000 a month extra income part time by using smart techniques in their spare time on the weekends.

One art dealer I knew, started out by just visiting antique dealers, and flea market dealers and would research their art, and then he would make a deal to sell the art, for them, for a commission, and then he would market the art, to another dealer, and reap huge rewards.

There are many art dealers that work from their homes, and have many works of art in lower volume local auctions every month. These works of art were discovered at garage sales, yard sales and flea markets. And they were purchased for very little money as little as $20 each. Every month this part time weekend art dealer would generate 3 to 5 thousand dollars a month, in flea market, dealer, auctions, and direct sales.

In my travels I used to remember many art dealers who would take many months off, as a vacation to go to exciting places, and exotic countries looking for art treasures. The money they made from their art dealing adventures gave them and their families a wonderful life.

I always liked hearing from them after they got back, as they always had amazing stories of places they had been, and they looked very happy to get back to their art dealing businesses.

In this book, I have put together many of the techniques used by successful weekend part time art dealers, that I have had the honor to meet over the last 30 years. Most of them are just like you, and they all just simply had the same love of art, artists, and taking that love and making very successful businesses.

Everyone has art on their walls, why can it not be real original human made art? There is such an appreciation of this real art, that was created from a real artist. And if you stick with this art dealing everyone has met a significant contributor artist to the world of human art on Earth.

You will meet them also, and might even be a market maker for them, it is a very exciting and fulfilling way to make some extra profits, in only a very short amount of time.

You can do it too!

Are you ready for your art adventure?

Top Secret Technique 2
How to set up your Art Dealer Reference Desk, Library and Art Gallery in your home

1. Decorate with your artworks you have for sale.

2. Have a special place with a nice flat table to examine your artworks thoroughly.

3. Your art reference library should be extensive.

4. You should have a computer to assist you in research and in emailing photographs for evaluation.

5. You should have a digital camera for further evaluation and to send pictures to potential customers.

6. You should have tools for removing nails and doing simple repairs.

7. Cotton and cleaning solutions help also because you do not know what you will be dealing with in the condition of the work of art.

8. You should have letterhead, envelopes and business cards like any business. Also get a journal so that you can document your Art adventures, appointments, phone numbers and make notes about your Art research.

9. There should be some packaging material and maybe labels for shipping.

10. Lots of auction catalogs and a radio or CD player for plenty of fine music, and browsing during your art research adventures!

11. Purchase a very good loupe or magnifying glass.

12. Buy a black light for signature verification and over painting analysis.

13. Get a very high resolution video camera, digital camera, or a very good mobile phone camera, as today the mobile phone can be an invaluable tool for the art dealer. Also the mobile phone can access research tools like The Art Signature File on Kindle, that where you can download the Kindle app and check art out by the artists signatures on your mobile phone.

14. Another use for a mobile high resolution camera in your mobile phone is that you can snap pictures of fronts and backs of art, and take a picture of the signature, and you can look up the signature, outside in your car, in The Art Signature File, by G.B. David Kindle version to decide if the art has a value.

15. By having the Kindle app installed on your mobile phone you can also get the Kindle version of this book 101 Top Secret Techniques Used by Successful Part Time Weekend Art Dealers, which you can use the built in price guide as a research tool also.

Top Secret Technique 3
Old Art is not always the only art that has a value

Some think that an artwork must be old to be valuable. In other words, you must have an old master work of art if you want it to be of value! This is not true in the fluid art world we live in today. The artist Yves Klein painted in the 1960's and his paintings can go in the millions. Franz Kline has million dollar sales records also. Of course we all know about Jasper Johns and his million dollar prices for his art at auction, even his prints or multiples have sold for $200,000. These are not old works of art and believe it or not contemporary artworks, are out there and easier to be discovered by the weekend art dealer.

A good example of that is the story of the contemporary work of art that was found, laying on a clothing table at a rummage sale. Nobody was interested in this work of art and they left it alone because it was very modern looking. People think unless it looks old that it cannot be worth much. At that sale that day fortunately there was a young art dealer who had studied modern art and was well learned. She immediately picked it up and purchased it for 75 cents. It was later sold at auction for $100,000! This is a true story, hard as it is to believe!

Like the contrarian stock pickers on Wall Street, who bet on the opposite of the trend, this young lady was making her own destiny and direction. While the entire world was looking for Old Master and Cows in a pasture beautiful paintings she was looking for those abundant creative works of art by the struggling artists of our modern and contemporary world!

Even today currently contemporary art created only 7 to 10 years ago is being auctioned at very high values. I also have included many current high prices of art that have sold recently at the end of this book, so that you can get a look at what's going on, and get an idea about the opportunities there are available in art dealing.

Modern and Contemporary art is very exciting and different, and today in the markets it is one of the most desired artworks that knowledgeable dealers are looking for. You should also know that the work of art the young brilliant woman discovered in the thrift sale was from 1938. The amazing thing about new looking art is that sometimes its actually not really new. It holds it's modern look throughout all the years in art and modern design and architecture.

Sometimes it's good to be a little out of the edge of the envelope in art collecting and art dealing in the fast changing fine art world! Try it, you will be pleasantly surprised in the rewards achieved utilizing this simple technique when you are on your art adventures!

Top Secret Technique 4
Artists Multiple Prints have a great value and resale value also

In the 1970's many artists created multiple prints, etchings and sculpture. Of course Picasso was doing this with his ceramics in the 1950's. And Hiroshige was making multiple woodblock prints hundreds of year's earlier in Japan. The average person that has any interest today thinks that a multiple print does not have any value. They think that only original works of art are valuable. Mainly they think this way because there is only one original work versus the multiple editions that prints have.

The amazing thing about these multiples is that they do have a value, but it is to a lesser value than the original work by the artist. The Art Signature File is a great source for for signatures and prices of valuable artists and lists a lot of the contemporary and modern print artists and their general values. This area is a great and valuable area for the weekend art dealer. There is actually a liquid value to some prints by known artists. And believe it or not Sotheby's and Christies fine art auction houses actually sell fine art multiple prints at very high prices.

Just remember this is a secret idea and fortunately not everybody knows this. That is why you can still go to a garage sale and buy a print worth $100 to $2,500 every weekend in America. The public has the misconception that if it's printed it is worthless!

Example Print Auction Record Sales:

James McNeil Whistler (1834-1903) Yellow House,
 Lannion Litho tint in colors
Sold for $107,200 April 2001

Cindy Sherman (b. 1954) Untitled (#92), 1982
Color coupler print Sold for $259,000 November 2000

Edvard Munch (1863-1944) Mädchen auf der Brücke,
1920 Woodcut with lithographic coloring
Sold for £278,750 December 2000

Sarah Lucas (b. 1962) Fighting Fire with Fire 6
Pack, 1997 six black and white photographs with
ink and acrylic Sold for £135,750 February 2001

Henry Moore (1898-1986) Three Female Figures,
circa 1950 Collotype printed in colors
Sold for £17,625 July 2000

Albrecht Dürer (1471-1528) Knight, Death and the Devil, 1513 Engraving Sold for £113,750 June 2000

Henri Matisse (1869-1954) La Danse, 1935-6 Monotype in colors Sold for $204,000 October 2001

Thomas Struth (b. 1954) Pantheon, Rome, 1992 CIBA chrome print Sold for $270,000 May 2000
Other Current Print Prices

Pierre Auguste Rodin print $19,200
Georges Braque print $20,000
Jacque Villon print $12,500
Marc Chagall print $34,375 - $156,000
Marc Chagall print $37,500
James Ensor print $22,000
Max Ernst print $7,800
M.C. Escher print $50,000
George Grosz print $10,625
after Henri Matisse print $40,625
Friederich Hundertwasser print $28,125
Jasper Johns print $218,500
Martin Lewis print $16,250
Roy Lichenstein print $86,500
Ernst Ludwig Kirchner print $17,500

Benton M. Spruance print $38,400

Henri Matisse print $34,375

James McNeil Whistler print $21,250

Joan Miro print $68,500

Claude Monet print $28,000

Robert Motherwell print $100,000

Rembrandt old master print $24,000

Piranesi old master print $15,000

Pablo Picasso print $194,500

Jackson Pollack print $102,000

Robert Rauschenberg print $35,000

Man Ray print $37,500

Charles Sorlier after

Andy Warhol 10 prints $1,426,500

Tom Wessellmann print $122,500

Top Secret Technique 5
Are You Crazy? You Can't Make Money Doing That!

Most people would think that you could not make money being an art dealer on the weekend. This is not a true statement, if you know what you are looking for, know how to buy it at the right price, and can sell it at a better price then you can make money doing this, and become an art dealer. The difference between Madison Avenue art dealers and you is only the size of the deals, but do not diminish the value of the small deal. Woolworths made a fortune selling 5 and 10 cent items, and buying a $20 painting and selling it for $200 is no different.

It's all about you, and using the techniques that are included in this book, along with a great network of other dealers, experts, artisans, and craftsmen. Today many people are buying works of art, and collecting them until they go up in value, and then flipping them for a nice profit. Art is even considered a security like a stock in India and Russia, and is traded like that. Also another reason that art is so hot now, is that there are fine art funds where investors have invested money so that when art is available it can be bought and sold at a higher price.

As a matter of fact art as an investment is currently outperforming the S&P 500 of stocks, for the last few years!

And Art is currently being considered as a must have as a hedge to monetary issues, and should be included in all portfolios of investment. Valuable art is everywhere, and is constantly being discovered. Art is difficult for the average person to determine what it is worth.

With a little knowledge you can very quickly sometimes identify valuable works of art. All it takes is just a willingness to research and view actual works of art in Auctions, Galleries, and Museums. By doing this we learn every day more and more about the identification of art. Having a book like The Art Signature File by G.B. David can help you identify works of art, by a signature, and it helps you evaluate the prices.

There are many research books that can make you a better art buyer and dealer. The world of Art Dealing is a secret world, and most people never know what art is sold and for what price in the world of art. The highest prices are never known to the world. Learn to identify what is really important in a work of art, the style, the subject, the way it is presented, the age of the paint, the paper, the support of the art, how it is framed then take all the information and make a good decision, and you will be on your way to a real adventure.

And one day soon, if you follow the techniques in this book you might find something that is a real art treasure. They are out there now, and they can be found. It happens every day, and people are cashing in. With the right knowledge, you can do it, anyone can do it!

Top Secret Technique 6
The Baby Boomer Art Gold Rush!

There is a current phenomenon going on right now that makes art dealing and art acquisitions particularly a good field to be in right now. There were seventy-six million American children were born between 1945 and 1964. Of those 76 million people some have 2 or more parents that are over 80 years old that were born at the top of the modern and contemporary art period of development. That means that many of these 140 million people will be giving, leaving to their baby boomer children, and throwing out a magnificent collection of works of art from every corner of the world, as they move into more manageable environments.

This phenomenon is starting right now, and as the price of real estate stays high, these types of things are happening faster. This is due to most baby boomers being into modern and new not used things, and not having the desire to keep these works of art their parents loved, collected, held onto all those years. So this thing is about to start, and many weekend art dealers have seen this in practice, as many times you will go to a sale and discover things that the children have no interest in.

As an example one time I was looking through some letters and photographs at a sale where a nice old lady had her children deal with her house after she went into a nursing home.

The house was disarrayed, and it looked well lived in, so I went into a home office area, and I noticed a drawer with letters, so I asked one of the children if it was ok that I look through the letters, and photos as I collect unusual photos, and they said it was ok as they were clearing the house out so they could sell the house.

So I found many photos of carnivals and fairs, and lots of family pictures which the family did not want to keep. And then I found this one photo of President Abraham Lincoln with a letter to a military officer, from him. This really amazed me so I picked out some drawings, and a couple of paintings, and when I went to check out with the person running the sale, and obvious family member, I said how much for these pictures, she said how about $20, and then I said what about these old letters and photos? She said "you really want those old things? If you really want those old letters then how about $5?" I said OK but these two items you should keep in the family, and showed them the photo of Abraham Lincoln and the letter he wrote obviously to one of their distant family members in the civil war around the late 1800's.

They were amazed at my generosity and my letting them know about that, and they gave me a small western cowboy oil painting about 8 inches by 10 inches as a gift, which I was able to later sell at auction for $500, after I researched it!

Top Secret Technique 7
Art can be found everywhere

Do you know how many times people have said, "All the artworks that are important have been discovered already" This is an amazing concept from the minds of people who could talk themselves out of doing most any worthwhile things. Believe it or not there are amazing amounts of works of art available on the streets, attics and the strangest places yet to be discovered. It stands to reason that not everything can be discovered ever! Because of the simple fact of human nature, we will not all do something all at the same time so how can all the works be discovered. Also not everyone knows everything.

An example given from one weekend art dealer couple was that they sold a group of paintings and prints they felt were not of any significant value to another dealer. Now you must know that these art dealers were experts in the modern artist period of art. They were selling this group of works of art to raise some money for another deal they were trying to make. They got $2,500 for the art that they had felt had decorative value.

After the sale, about a week later the person they sold these decorative works of art to, informed them that he was very upset with the art dealers, because they did not tell him that one of the works of art was worth $10,000! It seems that the person that the second art dealer sold the decorative works to then proceeded in selling some of the works to someone else who checked out one of the watercolors that actually had a gallery label on the back. He simply just called the gallery and inquired about the artwork. The smart art person then visited the gallery and was told that it was a valuable work of art by Jamie Wyeth related to Andrew Wyeth walked away with a $10,000 check! This is a true story!

Which brings up another painful aspect of art dealing, the after the sale testimony of how stupid you were in selling a valuable work of art to someone, for very little without thoroughly checking out the art you are selling! If they actually ever let you know!

Do not get into ever this situation, always research your works of art well. Try to understand what the work of art is illustrating. Get into the artists head, and try to see why the artist created the work. If I would have just looked at the art work, and thought about it, rather than thinking it was too modern to be valuable, I might have researched the signature in my Art Signature File at that time, later on I saw he was listed in the reference guide. My consolation in this mistake I made was that my friend also made the same mistake.

Remember "Not Everyone Knows Everything!" also "Not Everyone Knows the Value of Everything!"

Top Secret Technique 8
Buy any Abstract works of art dated between 1900 and 1950

If you discover any abstract works of art with a legitimate date between the years 1900 and 1950 it is probably important, or it should be. During this time there were very few artists thinking in an abstract way, so it stands to reason that these works are exciting and wonderful.

As a matter of fact they actually become historical because there are so few of them that were made during these years. The Futurists were some of these kind of abstract artists. Some were soldiers in the world war one period between 1915 and 1917. Their works go for incredible prices at auction today.

You should also know that I feel the Russian and Eastern block country art works in the style of the 1914 avant garde is starting to heat up, and I think there might be thousands of works of fine art coming into the market very soon. These works have never had a very good sales record, but they are so very exciting, and if you can find any of the artworks by these suppressed very creative artists you will surely have a treasure in your hands.

There were many avant garde abstract painters that are being discovered today in many estates. People collected these works and tucked them away in drawers, only to be discovered years later. There are many Russian, German, French and American works from this period. They can be found in the form of sketchbooks, drawings, paintings works on paper, even sculpture!

In the styles of abstract art we know that Cubism was imported from Spain by a Spaniard. Futurism is strictly Italian: there is not a French name among its originators. Synchromism was brought into the world by Americans. Der Blaue Reiter (The Blue Rider) was Germans and Russians Der Blaue Reiter was a movement lasting from 1911 to 1914, fundamental to Abstract Expressionism.

And Impressionism, which, like all these other departures, has come to be looked upon as French, is incontrovertibly of English parentage. And as the name so eloquently states the Russian Avant Garde represents a huge amount of Russian works of art, tens of thousands of works, produced in 1914 when there were only farmers in the world. True, there is small credit due the inventor, but we should be thankful for these regions that produced these exceptional artists.

And if you can ever be fortunate to fall upon a Blaue Reiter work of art from 1911-1914 you will have discovered a very important treasure as many of the artists perished in the war. I always get excited when I see these works out there.

To me all of these works of art during this period are priceless, as we most likely will never see a time like that ever again in the history of art in the world!

Top Secret Technique 9
Old Master Paintings can still be discovered and acquired today!

Earlier we discussed the way people think that old art is more valuable than new art. Believe it or not most people think that an Old Master painting is almost impossible to acquire today. This channel of thought is because most people think they are rare and already in museums, or that if they did come available they would cost in the millions.

This is untrue thinking; the secret is that you can purchase quality fine old master paintings at very reasonable prices today. They can be purchased at auctions, and in many other areas. Imagine your weekend art dealer business could actually be supplier of old master paintings to the upscale decorating market!

Also be on the lookout for old master prints, as many books and manuscripts were illustrated with valuable old master art prints and they are showing up at thrift sales, and old used book stores, they make great investments.

Remember this is a secret and if everybody knew this old master market might get popular and the prices would rise rapidly. The value of these works is surely to rise over the next 20 years because they will become rarer once the secret gets out, I know many dealers that collect these works of art!

Top Secret Technique 10
How much should you offer for art at outside sales?

Ah... here is the ultimate, weekend art dealer question, "How Much to offer potential sellers". One weekend art dealer always offers $200 for any work of art whether it was worth a million or a thousand. I do not know why dealers do this, but I have actually witnessed this technique and it might have something to do with the idea that $200 is perceived to be a lot of money. Of course this amount would vary under different inflationary periods, if the cost of regular white bread in your area was $1.00 a loaf, then you would offer say $200. If the price was higher, the formula would be 200 x (the cost of regular white bread) = offer. Also they might do this because they do not know the value of the art they are looking at, as they need time to appraise the art, so they figure that out of 10 works of art 1 might be valuable, so they offer the $200, to acquire the artwork, and then later on evaluate the real value of the art.

Another successful weekend art dealer only likes to offer under $50, or 50 x (the cost of regular white bread) for most quality works she discovers, she does this technique as to not like to draw attention to the value of the works of art she purchases. And believe it or not she sometimes buys art because she likes it and not because she knows it is valuable. Her taste and instinct occasionally pay out royally!

Then there is the other art dealer that will walk into a tag sale, yard sale or garage sale and see one valuable work of art. He then proceeds to saying very loudly, "I will give you $10,000 for everything in this house!" Guess what, the people running the sale laugh and then think he is joking. But he says it again, this time more seriously.

The crowds of other shoppers start to look at this man and get very quiet, as he says "Who is running this sale I would like to make a $10,000 offer for everything!"

They realize that he is not kidding around so the people running the sale look at each other seriously and then they say, "Are you serious?" He reveals he needs to furnish his house and that this is a legitimate offer. They think for a while and then say fine, the sale is closed and he pays them, and makes a phone call to his moving people to remove the contents.

Mean while he takes a few works of art with him as he leaves especially the work of art worth double what he paid for the whole contents! This is a true story! I have actually witnessed this technique, and it was a very exciting thing to see indeed! It's a little ruthless, but there are many people who do not like to stand in line, or waste their time in their searches for art out there in the provinces. They take their art dealing business very seriously, and they are rewarded royally.

But then again it's up to you and your judgment in determining what a work of art is worth to you as an individual who has to resell it or you will wind up keeping it in your collection of art works. Generally it's best to get the seller to say what they want for the art, or collection of art works.

Many art dealers I have known like to buy many artworks in one purchase. I actually have seen many art dealers, who were lucky enough to be able to purchase complete collections from artists families, who had no interest in their artist relatives works of art. Sometimes they even had appraisers who determined the artist never had sold at auction, or in any galleries, so they priced the artworks very low.

To me this is a very serious misjudgment, as I believe, an art collection should stand on it's own. A huge collection was discovered of the works of an writer artist who was a recluse, very few people ever knew he was an artist, and he painted for many years, and was only discovered after he passed away. In 1930, Henry Darger moved into a second-floor room on Chicago's North Side.

It was in this room, more than four decades later, after his death in 1973, that Darger's extraordinary secret life was discovered. Today, he is best known for his "outsider art," meaning those who have little contact with society or those who never received any type of formal art or writing lessons. His works go for up to $80,000

Top Secret Technique 11
How do you tell the difference between prints and drawings, and original art?

It is very important to tell the difference between a printed work on paper and an original unique drawing on paper. The main reason is the value judgment. A Print that has photo mechanically produced "dots" has a lesser value than an original drawing. Incidentally a small drawing by Henri Matisse can be worth over $200,000.

The reason for the value difference is simple. A photo mechanical print can have millions of copies, but a drawing is a onetime unique work of art. That is not to say that some artists may use the photo mechanical process to make limited editions that have a nice value. Most of these are signed and numbered with the edition. A Lithograph, is another form of print, they do not have photo mechanical dots. They are continuous tone in nature like an ink drawing. You can tell the difference by using a 10x or a 20x loupe magnifier looking at the ink and if it looks flat it could be printed.

Generally an ink drawing has all sorts of imperfections in the strokes of the pen. India ink seems to be a little raised. Jasper Johns lithographs have gone for more than $200,000.

Pencil on a drawing when the paper is turned at an angle has a silver shimmer. This is a good technique when looking at the back of an old wooden stretcher of a painting. Just tilt the wood with the light and look at the reflection off the darkened wood an obscure pencil inscription or a signature can sometimes be seen using this technique.

Remember when you are using your digital camera for analysis, to tilt these areas the same as you did with your eye before you snap the shot. You will be amazed at the results that you get when you see the pix!

I have a print and I want to know if it is original. It is very difficult, even impossible, to make this kind of judgment call without seeing the work in person. Research begins by consulting a catalogue raisonne (listing of all of an artist's prints), if one has been published for the artist in question.

The standard index to these specialized and very useful reference works is: Timothy Riggs, Index to Oeuvre-Catalogues of Prints by European and American Artists, New York, 1983. This text will lead you to the standard catalogues. In some cases the catalogue will include information about copies and forgeries.

If you cannot locate a copy of the catalogue raisonne suggested by Riggs (check your local art museum library) then it is possible that someone on prints will have access to the work and will be able to help you out. Research your art, it really gives you an edge on the competition.

An on-line addendum to Riggs (and eventually the integral text plus the addendum) is available at the Print Council of

America website. The texts listed below can also help determine some common kinds of facsimiles.

On old prints you sometimes find abbreviations taken from Latin or French words.

he or she painted it pinx (pinxit)

painted by del. (delincavit)

designed by inv. (invenit)

invented by fec. (fecit)

made by sculp. (sculpsit)

engraved by inc. (incisit)

engraved by exc. (excudit)

published by imp. (imprenit)

printed by (dessinee par)

designed/painted by (grave par)

engraved by impr. (imprime)

Another research technique I have used involves Ultraviolet light, or "black light", which reveals changes in elemental composition on the surface of objects because it causes specific fluorescence in materials depending on composition and age. Retouching, over painting, varnishes, adhesives, and certain types of deterioration that might be invisible to the naked eye, like mold damage, can be detected and identified. UV fluorescence can sometimes make erased ink visible, can indicate over painting or retouching, and can help identify different types of stains. For example, oil stains fluoresce orange, wax or starch can be bluish or unsized paper deep purple.

Different types of mold stains fluoresce differently, so even the kind of mold attack might be identified. Often mold attack is apparent in UV fluorescence even when it is completely invisible in normal light. Another tool is Infrared reflectography reveals carbon containing materials and otherwise "invisible" medium. Carbon media hidden under retouching, dirt, or other media can be seen, revealing under drawings or pentimenti (literally changes in thought), or render other media invisible, such as bistre inks. Infrared illumination is especially useful with some drawing media.

It can reveal covered signatures, or erased pencil and ink, or abraded or faded drawings. It can even penetrate paint layers to show primatura, or preliminary drawings. Magnification: In addition to illumination, magnification is a useful and relatively simple means of examining an object. A magnifying glass can often help to identify inclusions in paper or the type of media. However, sometimes much higher magnification is required for identification.

Top Secret Technique 12 Video and Digital Camera Research Tips

Here is a useful secret technique: Most Video camera's can be turned into an art research tool. A video camera equipped with a special infrared filter can see through the over painting on paintings and works on paper. It's amazing but I have actually done it myself. The technique is actually called infrared reflectography and here is how it's done; most video cameras, have a low light or below sensitivity ability, and can see in the dark. They actually can see infrared invisible light reflection. This means these cameras can see things our eyes cannot see.

Here is the technique simply described:

1. You first take an infrared filter and put it over your camera lens (Kodak has an infrared gelatin filter).

2. Next you get a true infrared light (most hardware stores have the inexpensive bulb and fixture).

3. You will need a tripod to keep your video camera still.

4. There are a couple of ways to proceed, one way is to shine the light on the front of the painting as you record the painting this will show you the under

drawing of the painting or work on paper. Another technique is to shine the light through the back of the artwork. This warms the base of the artwork and the camera sees the warm infrared base therefore it sees the under paint surface.

5. Be careful, as the infrared light can get very hot. Infrared cameras see the invisible spectrum of light we cannot see, so you actually see below the oil paint to the base of the canvas or paper base.

6. Then you can view your videotape and learn about the painting. I have actually been able to see a painting painted over another painting using this technique. Museum conservators use this technique for restoration and historical learning of what the artists thinking was about as they were creating their work of art.

One last thing that you should know, I have had museum conservators actually do infrared reflectography for me in some of my research, and it is very costly between $300 and $1,200! This is why I use this previous technique to research art, it is inexpensive and it's kind of fun seeing signatures and the under drawing or paintings under paintings!

I actually had a museum conservator give an opinion once on a work of art I was researching, and he said it was a master artist who painted the picture, just by observing the underdrawing. It turned out to be a very valuable work of art!

Top Secret Technique 12B
The Digital camera is also a great tool for the Art Research person

You can take a picture quickly and analyze it on the spot.

1. Take a picture of your art
2. Then open it in your picture editor (Gimp, and Microsoft Composer has great analysis tools and Adobe Photoshop is the best)
3. When you look at a photo of your art, sometimes you will see things that you did not notice, as you look at the art itself. Details can be more evident, and the perspective of how you look at the art is more distant generally.
4. Next you can increase contrast, lighten, darken etc. Alter the photo to see further aspects of the art.
5. Close up photos of the signature can help in the identification of the artist who created the work. Again sometimes the signature is faded, old, smeared, or covered with old varnish. Your contrast adjustments and the various color filters your picture editor has built in can increase the clarity for viewing.
6. On the back of old stretchers sometimes the artist will title the artwork in pencil. Pencil can be hard to read

sometimes. The digital camera can take a picture at different light angles that will reflect the shiny silver lead pencil for identification. Of course contrast and brightness adjustments help in viewing here also.

7. Digital photos can be used for insurance purposes, expert evaluation, or just to show you friends.

8. Most art auction companies are now taking digital photos for appraisal of art for their auctions today, so good clear photos can be emailed to anywhere on the planet for possible sale of your art.

9. Megapixels (MP) represent the number of dots in an image; the more megapixels, the higher the resolution. High resolution means more detail and a greater potential for cropping in on the details of your artwork. A 5MP or up to 12MP camera works great for photographing artwork.

10. A steady tripod for photographing art.

11. A good lighting system can be just 2 lights at 45 degree angles.

12. A black light which is used to identify restoration, new paint added, repairs, and signatures added to an art work. The newly added paint or cracks, or restoration appears black, over the old paint which appears grayish. Also Touch ups and restorations, torn paintings repaired can be seen under a black light very clearly.

Top Secret Technique 13
Pick up Used Auction and
Gallery Catalogs

A very useful tool for the weekend art dealer is the knowledge to know what to look for. By knowing what is valuable in the art world you can know what can be found in your local community world. Also, you might save some cash resources by not making as many mistakes. One way of accomplishing this knowledge goal, is a kind of interesting technique.

Every season the large auction houses have used catalogs with prices and full color pictures in them. These catalogs become abundant after the season is over and they sometimes are discarded or sold for around $3.00 to $7.00. They originally sell for $20.00 to $50.00 and some dealers and collectors actually have $3,500 subscriptions to these catalogs yearly.

You can see them up for sale on Ebay, local flea markets, and at the 26th street flea market in New York City. You can also find these old auction catalogs on Craigs list. And recently the auction sites of the largest art auction houses have a huge database of the works of art they are selling. I find it a pleasure to scroll through the works of art that come up for sale, sometimes I actually see works that I have sold years ago that come up at auction occasionally.

Every topic of collecting is represented and you can choose your subject. Sotheby's and Christies have the 2 best groups of catalogs. But I have discovered Ader Tajan, located in Paris France, Butterfields, located in California and Bonhams, in England and various other exotic area catalogs with great info also.

You should acquire these catalogs for your art library and look through them often, as they are the best example of visually and monetarily what is selling at the current auction market. There are so many small auction houses all over the world, and the art in these smaller venues is sometimes art that has never been seen before. The art sold by these auctions comes from the actual estates of people, and smaller art dealers use these auction places to sell their excess inventory.

You can learn quite a bit about art, artists, and the sales process browsing through old auction catalogs, and see how the trends in art sales have changed over the years. At the same time by surfing the large auction houses upcoming auctions you can understand the value of the artworks out there, and see de-accessioned museum works of art that can go at lower prices, buying here is sometimes fruitful.

Of course one day you will have a great work of art up for sale at one of these art auction houses. And your picture of your work of art and a description will be in there also!

One can only work hard for this day!

Top Secret Technique 14
Pick up Used Art Magazines

Any art magazine is a wealth of the current information at the time of the publishing, the older the magazine the better, not to say that current magazines have a tendency to keep an art dealer up on the current trends in art. Old copies can be bought through ebay, and http://www.biblio.com, also thrift stores, church sales, library sales and anywhere where old magazines are liquidated, are great places to discover art research magazines.

Estate sales, garage sales and tag sales are exceptionally good places to get old magazines, I have actually been fortunate enough to be at the right place and the right time of a sale that was an art collector who was moving over seas and had to dispose of their magazine collection, and was able to get a full magazine collection for only $300 some of the magazines were from 1930's 40's and 1950's, which gave me the knowledge of some great art movements.

Many galleries have placed ads for shows with images of art, and I actually discovered some serious provenance for a work of art I was researching through one of these magazines!

Also Google has many magazines and books that you can read, and also here at http://www.archive.org/ are websites from the past. You can see a 1920's Print Connoisseur magazine that has invaluable information about prints. All of these periodicals can make an art dealer an expert in the past art articles subjects and makes for a better decision process in buying, and researching art.

At the end of this book there is a complete and very good, comprehensive list of art magazines that can still be found and that have an enormous amount of art information that will help you in your art adventures!

Also you can go to: http://www.pastpaper.com

http://archive.org/search.php?query=print%20connoisseur%20AND%20mediatype%3Atexts

The Print Connoisseur provided subscribers with a quarterly journal that focused on artists producing etching, woodcuts, lithographs, and engravings. Each issue included an original piece of art, many of which were commissioned for that issue. Published under the direction of Winfred Porter Truesdell

In 2006, a complete index was published by Alan Wofsy Fine Arts with the names of all artists who's artworks were published during the period 1920-1932.

https://books.google.com/books/about/Print_Connoisseur.html?id=dTk3AAAACAAJ

Top Secret Technique 15 Spend some time in Art Museums

One of the best places to learn about art, is actually in an art museum, there you can see the art and get used to its styles and the way it is formed. You would be amazed at how many times you see a work of art in a 2 dimensional book, and it looks totally different in the 3 dimensional real world museums.

So it will help you as a weekend art dealer to be familiar with art of any form. This is all because you never know what you will discover. The art exhibits in the museum range from the internal collection to the traveling exhibitions.

Traveling exhibitions allow us a better visual sense of art not seen anywhere else. Sometimes the art in the traveling exhibitions is also art that has very low sales records, kind of a future fine art auction collection.

From these obscure collections sometimes real superstar artists emerge, but then there are some that never get a fine art sales record. At any rate these exhibitions are important for the real weekend art dealer to learn with and to help develop their collection ideas!

Also I have personally found the curators of art museums are very approachable during your art research, they have actually helped in solving many art mysteries. The museum library is incredible in its scope of material. There are exhibition catalogs, catalog Raisonne's and much more to choose from!

Here are some great resources:

Heilbrunn Timeline of Art Compiled by the Metropolitan Museum of Art's curatorial, conservation, and education staff, covers pre-history to the present day. Contents arranged chronologically, geographically, and thematically

Oxford Art Online Search across several authoritative art encyclopedias and dictionaries, including the Benezit Dictionary of Artists, Encyclopedia of Aesthetics, Oxford Companion to Western Art, and The Concise Oxford Dictionary of Art Terms.

Grove Art Online includes 45,000 signed articles on every aspect of the visual arts, with more than 23,000 subject entries and 21,000 biographies.

Getty's Union List of Artist Names Each artist record includes biographical information, names (including given names, pseudonyms, variant spellings, married names, etc., with one name flagged as the preferred name), related artists, notes, and citations. Covers antiquity to the present; international in scope.

Clara: Database of Women Artists From the National Museum of Women in the Arts. The "custom search" allows searching by country/state of origin and residence.

Top Secret Technique 16
Go to Art Gallery shows

The Art Gallery show is an excellent source for learning about art. The art gallery will have an opening of a new show occasionally to show the artist works that they represent. They usually have refreshments, and information about the art that is being shown, and about the artists. The director is there to answer any questions you have and the art investing and collecting patrons are there also. It's a nice time for all that collect, enjoy, and profit from art. The gallery will sometimes also have prints and graphics, plus prices for all the artworks are available also. The gallery often has a reading library for additional reference for patrons, and interested art researchers.

What the art gallery also offers the weekend art dealer is a place to sell art. Many art deals have been made in direct negotiations with the art gallery. It's a very simple procedure, all you do is determine which art gallery specializes in your particular work of art. Then you offer the work of art to that gallery. The advantage is that the art gallery knows the street market value of that work of art. They also know the history and the future value of the art.

Believe it or not you can sometimes get a higher price than from any other sources quickly from an art gallery! Many times the label on the back of a work of art is a gallery label. If it is an art gallery label, this can make your marketing of that work of art easy. There are thousands of art galleries in the world and Art in America every year has a list that is very useful. It lists the art galleries and the artists they specialize in. This is a must have tool for the weekend art dealer!

Also another point is you meet many people who have an interest in art at galleries. And if you network with these people, they are buyers, collectors, other dealers, and gallery owners, and managers, so you can connect with valuable interesting people that can help you, or guide you along the way in your art dealer adventures.

Artsy is a great resource related to art galleries…

Artsy features the world's leading galleries, museum collections, foundations, artist estates, art fairs, and benefit auctions, all in one place. Their growing database of 350,000 images of art, architecture, and design by 50,000 artists spans historical, modern, and contemporary works, and includes the largest online database of contemporary art.

Artsy is used by art lovers, museum-goers, patrons, collectors, students, and educators to discover, learn about, and collect art.

Artsy is a place to explore current and past exhibitions at museums and galleries, biennials, and cultural events, and to preview international art fairs before their doors open to the public.

Top Secret Technique 17
Look for Art Auction Labels, and Gallery Labels

Labels on a work of art from art auction houses can sometimes be a great reference for the weekend art dealer. If you see a label on the back of a painting, mostly they are round in nature, you can assume unless it is from another work of art that it was in a sale at one of the larger art auction houses. This means that it must be important enough for the experts at that auction house to have auctioned it off. Also the label will have an auction number and with a little research you might even be able to get to the actual date and what it sold for at auction.

Here are some popular Art Auction houses:

Bonham's & Brooks

Butterfield & Butterfield

Christie's

Etude Tajan

Hodgins Art Auctions, Ltd.

Lunds Auctioneers and Appraisers, Ltd

Pacific Galleries, Inc

Phillips de Pury & Luxembourg

Sloan's Auctioneers and Appraisers

Sotheby's

Drouot - Paris

Zeller - Germany

Dorotheum Vienna

Quittenbaum – Germany

de Veres Art Auctions

Doyle New York

Beijing Poly

Heritage Auction Galleries

Hauswedell & Nolte

Ragu Arts and Auction Center

Tepper Galleries

Waddington's

Many weekend art dealers have used this technique to identify an otherwise unidentifiable work of art. You see the label is the key to what the work of art is.

Once you check with records of the sale, it usually will give the description of the artist and the provenance info. This technique comes in handy when it comes time to sell the work of art. Everyone likes to have a story about the work.

What I really like about knowing where an art work has been, or exhibited, when I visit the gallery, or have a conference call with a gallery, they are very helpful in telling me the provenance of the art, as they keep excellent records!

Top Secret Technique 18
Labels on an artwork can tell you nothing or everything about the artwork!

Labels can sometimes have gallery information on the back. This information can be useful, (one weekend art dealer actually sold a $10,000 work of art to a gallery on the back of a work of art!)

But there are those instances when some unscrupulous person has placed an important label on the back of a work of art to add to its importance. Always look at the age of the label and ask, "Does it match the age of the art?" also check out the gallery and try to see if the artwork was something of what the gallery might represent. If the label looks made up or fake there might be other things wrong with the art you are identifying.

When a label is placed on the back of a fine work of art it usually is placed carefully straight. Sometimes a label is placed for a particular exhibit. These labels might have the name of the artist and the title of the work. Match the title with what the art actually looks like, this does not always work, but it sometimes is a good quick technique.

Sometimes the identification is stamped on the canvas or backing of a work of art. If there are multiple labels this can mean that the work was exhibited many times and places.

Also if it has a German swastika, it might be a lost degenerate artist work, or a war work of art that was confiscated. Museum labels also show up on works of art discovered by weekend art dealers.

Museum, Exhibition or Gallery labels can mean one of 4 things

(1) The work of art was in a traveling exhibition and returned to the collector.

(2) The work was de-accessioned by a museum, (sold out of their collection).

(3) The work was stolen out of a museum.

(4) The work was presented to a museum for some purpose and they put a label on it then returned it to the person.

Generally when a work of art has a museum label on it this adds to the value of that item. But in some cases it could be an insignificant work of art by an obscure artist whose career never got anywhere and the museum sold the work. It's still worth pursuing the label research because most of the time a label is just that, a means to identifying the path that a work of art has traveled in the universe!

Top Secret Technique 19
How to tell if a Work of art is the Age it looks

There are many ways in determining the age of a work of art. First look at the date on it, determine if it could be from the year it has marked. Normally a painting, sculpture or work on paper will have the artist's signature or mark and a date, or it will have a date somewhere on the work. Of course this is not always true, because some artists just sign the work of art and do not date it. When you look at a canvas that is mounted on a stretcher, identify if it is attached with staples this generally means it is fairly new. This is because most canvases were attached to the stretchers before the 1920's with nails. Also on the subject of nails if they are new and shiny then that is another factor of age. As brown and rusty nails show that it could be old. An old nail's shape also is a factor, if the nail head is perfectly round then it is newer than if its head is odd shaped and more primitively made.

I have also found that an accomplished artist sometimes spaces his nails equal distance from each other of course this is not always true. Some artists will wrap their canvas in a hap hazard way around the stretcher as others will wrap it more precise.

Some 1900's painters had their canvases prepared by colorists so they were made very nicely. An old canvas really looks that way, the fake ones usually have to be colored with coffee or a stain to make them look old. Be aware of this possible deception, most likely you must develop a sense of the age of the canvas, as you view them often.

In your networking as a good weekend art dealer you should keep a mental database of the backs of paintings. Go to your local flea markets, garage yard sales and auctions. Turn over all potential works of art and try to identify the approximate year of creation. Touch the art and from the back see what you can see. If the painting on the front does not synchronize with the back it might fall into a suspicious area. By doing this even if you do not buy anything, you will be able to access your mental database for the time when you do buy.

Dating Sculpture requires a different dating process. Look at the medium is it bronze, metal, brass etc. Here's a secret, a bronze usually carries a much higher value in sculpture although this is not the rule. A marble work of art can also carry a much higher price, generally it's the complication of the process combined with the reputation of the artist.

An example would be that a Rodin bronze might be equal in price to a Brancusi marble sculpture, in some cases as the size and rarity sometimes determines the price of the work of art. Also how long the artist worked, how many works of art he produced, and if he was well received by the art community. An artist can also be a great innovator, but his technique might make his art look older than it actually is.

Three steps to identification

1. The front or face view
2. The back or build view
3. The microscopic laboratory view

When an art dealer looks at art he will most of the time use the 1 and 2 technique to view art, and the number 3 technique has to be used if the dating does not look right, or there is a question about the date of a work of art.

The 3rd technique is reserved for use by an art conservator in case an evaluation is needed to be determined. But normally looking at the front and back of an artwork is all that is needed in most cases of identification.

Also the edges of works of art help in determining age, by the nails in canvass, the layers of the surface paint, and identification of if the art has been modified. Always keep an open mind and do not instantly assume your first views are right. Always consider the possibility that the art could be a forgery. I knew a dealer who refused to purchase some works of art, by saying it just looks to right, too real.

Do not make this mistake, as that is exactly why my art dealer friend let a $10,000 work of art go for $100, it looked too real too good to be a valuable artist.

Also Japanese prints can be identified through this web site: Ukiyo-e.org

"The Ukiyo-e.org database and image similarity analysis engine, created by John Resig to aide researchers in the study of Japanese woodblock prints, was launched in December 2012. The database currently contains over 213,000 prints from 24 institutions and, as of September 2013, has received 3.4 million page views from 150,000 people."

"The database has the following major features:"

A database of Japanese woodblock print images and metadata aggregated from a variety of museums, universities, libraries, auction houses, and dealers around the world.

An indexed text search engine of all the metadata provided by the institutions about the prints.

An image search engine of all the images in the database, searchable by uploading an image of a print.

Each print image is analyzed and compared against all other print images in the database. Similar prints are displayed together for comparison and analysis.

Multiple copies of the same print are automatically lined up with each other and made viewable in a gallery for easy comparison.

The entire web site, and all artist information contained within it, is available in both English and Japanese, aiding international researchers.

Top Secret Technique 20
Ask people and look for any old paintings even, torn paintings!

When you are on your weekend excursions, always look for torn or damaged paintings. These can be a lucrative adventure for you. A very prosperous weekend art dealer makes most of his profits from these kinds of works of art. The principle of the idea is that when a painting is torn the owner generally thinks it is of no value or it will cost too much to restore it.

Actually there are many restorers that will work within your budget for the restoration process. Also if the restoration is excessive, you can research the painting and if it's by a well listed painter, the restoration house will sometimes partner the work for a share in the painting when it is sold. That way you the art dealer take none or less of the risk in a financial way. There are many restoration firms out there so ask around at your local art and antique auction houses for the ones they use or have heard of.

Restoration sometimes falls into your lap, either because the art is pretty but has no listed value, or the artwork is destroyed too far to have value.

Let's say if the artwork has all of the painting gone except one cow in a pasture.

Here is what one successful weekend art dealer does. He will have someone paint in the background in the style of the artist and then he will sell it as decorative art, or just hang it on the wall for one's personal enjoyment.

Remember do this at your own risk, because personally if I could prove that cow was painted by Picasso I feel it would still be worth a lot to a collector! Sometimes a piece of art by an artist is in big demand, so do not look down on torn, damaged, water damaged works of art.

There are many fragments from the Egyptian era that have noses missing, cracked tiles, that today are priceless. Give me a Jasper Johns work of art from his burned period in the beginning of his career, and I will show you how to get thousands for that art.

A Jackson Pollock drip painting from the 40's with a tear, or even a chunk missing is priceless today. And you should know I do not believe restoration of these chards of paintings or works of art gain value with restoration. Sometimes it's better to just leave the art alone, and preserve it in a frame.

So go out there and save all the torn works of art that wind up in dumpsters all over the world because people like to have perfect art on their walls. You will be rewarded for the abundance these works of art bring to your collection, and to the art historical communities, and it makes a great conversation piece for your next art dealer meet up that you have started or attended!

Top Secret Technique 21
Always have at least $100 cash on you to spend at sales

Always have available when you are on a weekend art excursion at least $100 in cash in your pocket. This is the advice of one part time art dealer that has lost the opportunity to purchase nice works of art because she had to go to the cash machine and the seller changed their mind or sold it to another person while they were gone. It goes something like this, you are out at estate sales, yard sales, or garage sales, and you see a work of art lying on the floor in front of your feet. It has the look of the kind of art you like and want. But as you pick it up, because you look intelligent the owner starts to like the item more and more, thinking you might have a valuable work of art.

Now all of a sudden the owner is thinking about keeping the painting. But, because they are embarrassed about pulling it away from you they give you a price. You negotiate a slightly better price by pointing out the tear, paint missing, damaged frame or restoration points and the owner then starts to feel maybe its not worth what they thought so they give you a great bargain price.

This is where you reach into your pocket and to your dismay you only have $40 in cash. "Oh can you hold the painting for me I have to go to the cash machine you then say". As you are leaving the seller puts the picture under a table as they view it thinking maybe it is worth something after all, if you are willing to go all the way to the cash machine, it might be something of value.

When you return with the money, they tell you "Oh, I am so sorry my husband accidentally sold the painting to another person while you were gone for more than your offer". This happens quite a lot to dealers, so make sure when you are making deals, to be able to close the deal as soon as you make it. Bring extra cash with you on your treasure excursions!

Remember "Perceived Value" If we observe another person valuing an object by showing interest in it, picking it up, observing it, caressing it, it's "perceived value" goes up in our thinking.

The instant someone else wants something, its "perceived value" goes up like in auctions, auction fever etc.

The inside feeling to take it from them can come from either wanting to possess the value ourselves or from taking the value away from the other person even though the buyer or seller doesn't value the object at all.

Top Secret Technique 22
Three Important Words, Research, Research, Research!

Once a couple of weekend art dealers were clearing out their inventory of paintings that they could not sell, so they invited an antique dealer they knew to come to dinner, one night and the antique dealer wanted to buy some paintings for her store from the art dealers. As they were looking at the paintings the antique dealer saw a few that were of interest so they made a deal for 25 paintings for $2,500.

This is how the antique dealer liked to buy, not just one item but several, hoping to get at least one that was worth the trip. After about a week the antique dealer came back to the part time art dealer and was very upset. He had sold some of the 25 paintings that he purchased, and a customer who bought one of the paintings for $100, came back to him and said "Thank You! You made my day! I just sold that watercolor for $10,000"

As amongst the 25 paintings was a small marine watercolor, painted by the artist Jamie Wyeth that was worth $10,000! After buying the watercolor, and taking it home, the customer looked on the back and saw a gallery label and called the gallery on the phone.

The gallery then asked them to bring it in, so they could identify it. They cut a $10,000 check for it the very next day after the person bought it for $100! Unfortunately the antique dealer did not check out the painting, as he thought that the weekend art dealer he bought the 25 paintings had checked them all out already, because of the low price he paid for them. This was an example of two art dealers that did not do their research and everyone lost out, except for the delighted smart customer.

I have always found the research of art works to be a very rewarding activity. Many times I learned who the artists were, and why they created their works of art. This always gave me an incite into who these very creative artists, and it always brought out things I had never known about them, and the groups they associated with.

Some times if a style of art is researched of an art work, many things become clear, which make it possible to prove, and from there you can then go to the what if this is really by one of the artists of that genre, period, or technique.

In the weekend art dealer business, "if you snooze you lose", you cannot be lazy, and you must check out things thoroughly. Obviously the antique dealer trusted that the art dealer knew what they were doing. But in this case it did not get caught until the third party had the brilliance to check it out, as he was a smart professional art dealer!

Top Secret Technique 23
Get to know your art dealer competition

One weekend art dealer has discovered that networking with your competition can help you learn, save time and money, and lead you in the right direction in your art dealer business. Most part time and full time art dealers are the friendliest people. They often will give you valuable advice, and if they do not know, they will lead you to places that you can go to get the advice you need.

Your competition can be found standing in line at a thrift sale, at a flea market, at auctions plus many other places. These people are a valuable network for you, and you should pursue these relationships, as they can be very important in your art dealer business. Let's say you have a painting that needs to be restored.

You can call around and talk to the many restorers there are in the yellow pages, but this will not give you the personal experiences that other dealers have had with this restorer. By asking another art dealer who is a good art restorer you just might lead into more information that can be valuable to you.

Also a co-operative art deal can be beneficial to both parties involved. Maybe an art dealer might know a way, or have a connection to a customer that is looking for a particular work of art. If you work out a deal with all parties a difficult sale can be accomplished at a better price!

Get to know your competition, it can be lucrative for you plus because of like interests it can also be fun telling the many stories that art dealer's have to tell. Networking is lucrative, enlightening and good for your art adventures! You would be surprised how much you can learn from people that have the same likes as you do in art. Many techniques can be learned from other art dealers. I have found that the older the art dealer is the more they are willing to share with you.

Also I have found that many art dealer legends take a lot of their time with you, if you bring them an interesting work of art that you are researching. I believe they really love their art, and art in general. They look at your artwork, and they try to give you a direction to go if they can not identify it.

And I have taken works of art to well known art dealers in New York City, who have literally gotten very quiet when they have seen some of my artworks. As they can sometimes be stunned by the existence of some of the art treasures discovered more and more these days out there.

Meet ups, gallery shows, galleries, auctions and even artist studios are great places to meet other art dealers and collectors. You will see they will be very happy to converse with you, and talk about the one's that got away, or even techniques they have used in the past, it will be well worth your time in socializing!

Top Secret Technique 24
How to get the most cash for your art

Before you can work out a plan to get the most cash for your works of art, you must first determine what it is worth. It's a little complicated to understand the pricing of art, but once you get the pieces of the puzzle it all comes together. It's amazing how many times weekend art dealers have told me this story. They sold a work of art to someone for $100 who immediately sold it to someone else for $500 who then proceeded to sell it someone else for $2,500. This is a story that shows that art can sometimes have many different values.

So, what is the way to tell what art is worth? If you ask most weekend part time art dealers they will tell you to use an art reference book with sales prices. There are many of these available, Yearly art price books like Mayers, Art Sales Index, ADEC, etc. One great cumulative art reference is the Art Signature File, or Davenport's Art Price guide.

The difference between the yearly and the cumulative price guides are that the yearly shows prices for the previous year at auction, where the cumulative art price guide shows all the artists that have sold over the years.

Of course the Art Signature file is the only cumulative art price guide and signature specimen book. This helps you easily in determining the artist that created the work of art.

Having a cumulative book is great in a sense that sometimes an artist may not have sold anything at auction, so that year his listing would not be there. So you have to have quite a few years of books to be able to research right. They are now selling versions for 10 and 20 years of data that helps eliminate this problem. It goes this way; if you can afford only one resource go with a cumulative art price book. If you can afford more combine the cumulative with the yearly records. The yearly records have more advantages in the actual auction place, size of the artwork, and any particular techniques or supports are included.

Now we have a price guide to begin our research, but that is not the whole answer. Many people have spent a lot of time trying to devise systems to make pricing art like pricing tomatoes. It actually is kind of similar in a basic level. Remember art does go up and down in price kind of like tomatoes. If the farmer has an abundant year the price goes down, if the farmer has a bad year the price goes up. In art this is also possible. Say a fine artist died young, was part of a major art movement, and produced only a fraction of his potential in a lifetime.

His works would be very expensive. In the other sense if an artist pumped works out like a factory then his work would be less of a value.

Of course there are the exceptions to the rule, take an artist like Picasso, he had created so much art that when he passed away the people handling the estate were stepping all over it in his home. Does this mean his limited edition mass produced ceramics from the 1950's have low value? Some can go as high as $12,000! Andy Warhol produced beautiful serigraphs by others hands and did many multiple editions in the 1970's, his works dropped in value and are now selling at higher levels today!

So, many different factors are included when you determine the price of art but always understand that certain artist's have a popularity equation to be factored in. This popularity equation can be tracked effectively using these price guides. Another part of the puzzle is the historical or academic value of the particular work of art.

A work of art can be worth more than the price listed in an art auction price book, if it has a story. A story is explained in this way. Say you have a work of art and it fits into a collector's collection. He must have it so the price now can successfully go. Or maybe a museum needs the work of art to show a particular technique in its exhibits, this can make a work of art go for more than the actual listing.

There are always exceptions to the rules, which now lead us into the final aspect of getting the highest price. Should I sell at auction or sell the work privately? Selling at auction is easy you send your photo to the auction house you like. They say if they want it for their auction. You then ship them the picture, and in as much as 60 days to 12 months, you get payment minus the seller's premium 10% or more depending on the auction house. They also will charge a fee for taking a picture and putting it in their catalog.

It's nice and easy, but in contrast private sales have their advantages also, but it requires you to have patience, do more work, and get to the buyers. Of course this is what makes a great art dealer. The art dealer deals, remember when the art dealer does not deal, he kind of really isn't an art dealer. Not to say that a lot of weekend part time art dealers do sell most of their fine art works, through art auction houses. But once you broker your first art deal a magic spell gets cast over you and a whole new, world opens up.

Statistically, prices received for art at auction generally are much less than those prices gained at private sale. One reason that these prices are not published is that they are private. It's kind of an underground thing. The buyer has something fresh, (not shown around) the collector has a chance to purchase it before anyone else.

The collector knows if he does not act, it will surely be up at public auction, maybe he might get it for less but then at auction it might fly up in price!

It's gamble if you need to fill a collection. It's you and him, sometimes a check is cut no bargaining, but it can be just as exciting if there is bargaining, lets face it that's the fun of art dealing! And remember no one knows everything, during the bargaining process you may actually learn something you did

74

not know. Your price may have to be adjusted because of credible information the expert collector has as to the value.

To be truly successful in your art dealing business, you should always:

1.   Try to sell your better works privately then if this fails sell it at fine art auctions.

2.   Sell new artist's works and listed artists privately at your home gallery, of course more important works you can take to the customer.

3.   Liquidate mistakes and pretty pictures with no value utilizing online auctions like Ebay internet auctions or in sales.

4.   Trade works of art for services and for other works that might fit into your collection or your customers collections.

5.   Develop a want list with your art buying customers and be on the lookout for these works that are wanted.

6.   Secure a list of possible other art dealers that might buy from you and cultivate the list.

7.   Secure a list of antique dealers with stores that might buy from you and cultivate the list.

8.   Secure a list of ebay sellers that want to have artworks they can sell, and give them a great profit when they sell for you.

9.   Secure a list of decorators, and home furnishing stores that might want to buy art from you and cultivate the list.

10.   Secure a list of consignment shops, and keep them full of your art, and cultivate the list.

11.   Have plenty of business cards, and give them out to everyone, make them useful by printing both sides, and add an incentive for people to refer you to other people, like "10% referral fee for art sellers or buyers."

"Cultivate"

To grow or raise (something) under conditions that you can control, in our way of thinking, we want to start with a list and grow the list, so we can have an expanding business outlet for our art.

Top Secret Technique 25
Show your art to several people and create dialogue

Whether you are a collector or a dealer, showing your works to other people is a great Technique. For the collector, one can learn even more about people's perceptions of what they see. It's amazing how many people, no matter how much education or how well traveled an individual can be, they all have some sort of opinion when it comes to art.

When it comes to the weekend art dealer, there are times when we get stuck, and have a problem identifying our art. I have found that if you show your art to your friends and associates, they sometimes come up with constructive insights into the art.

One art dealer has actually no capabilities in being able to evaluate a painting by sight. She always uses other people's views on her art to get clues for the research. Some of the people she shows her art to are gallery directors, and museum people. It is interesting to note that even an unsigned work is viewed by these kinds of dedicated people with serious interest, as they see things in a work of art that we cannot even imagine.

Showing your art around is also a great way to get an insight into the people we associate with. I like to see how different people react to a work of art at a dinner party. It can make for a special conversation enhancer, and you would be surprised at some of the opinions of people! These opinions can sometimes lead to great discoveries. Also tip people well if their incite leads to a monetary gain in the dealing of art. Why not pay good people that have a good eye.

Another way to show your art is to exhibit it in cafes, restaurants, hotels, hospitals, spa's or golf clubs with price and website, email, or phone where local people can contact you for dialogue.

And still a great way to sell your excess artworks is to attend art shows, festivals, and flea markets. It is a good way to meet many local people, as 10's of thousands of people go to these street festivals and shows. You should always have business cards, and post cards showing that you not only sell art, but you buy art, you represent artists, and you can be an art consultant to investors, and people who are decorating with art.

Art is a great investment, and your knowledge is very needed for people to make good choices if they are buying art as an investment. It's all about socializing.

Always show your clients that they should buy art that is out of style for the best rewards, they should buy what they like as they may have to live with the art. Show them how buying lesser works can be important works down the road. And always remember to show them that there is a collectible market in artists works different from the larger market also.

Top Secret Technique 26
Have dinners for potential Art customers

Invite your customers and potential customers to dinner. This is a very useful technique that provides the opportunity for you to have your art that is for sale displayed. You also may have an interesting time, and the feedback you get for each artwork can help you in your future art business. You should have 20% new artist works that you represent, mixed in with your listed fine art works, also you should have a good mixture of styles and mediums for your customer to view.

Some weekend art dealers specialize in a particular style and period. This can actually work for the collector customer usually may collect a particular type of art. But having a well rounded collection to offer has its advantages. The dinner party customer may not be interested in some of your choices of art, but might have a friend who you can contact.

You need to network as much as you can. Another great aspect to the casual dinner party viewing is that the art customer knows you are in the business and that they might be there to purchase. But even if they do not see anything that they like, all will probably have a good time. Remember associating with people who have an interest in what you have an interest in is very exciting!

Top Secret Technique 27
Get to know an art conservator or restorer

The best Art restorers are hard to find, so getting to know, and working with a great art restorer is important. A bad restorer can cost you thousands in the final sale of your artwork. Where a good restoration job can mean many thousands and can extend the life of the artwork. Being on the good side of these magical people, might even get you a better price for the restoration!

Also most restoration people if they are very proficient at what they do, will have connections to buyers, collectors, museums, and auction houses, and can lead you in the right direction for marketing your artworks.

Here are some restoration prices for comparison:

Cleaning a small painting could run $150-$300, a Cleaning and Re varnish 30" x 25" could be $1000 to $2500, if the Frame needs work then it could run between $1500 and $3500. As you can see the prices are very high, and of course you should first identify the art before even considering the process of commissioning an art restoration project.

If you are restoring and cleaning and conserving, a painting that is being resold, consider that the new owner might want to use their conservator for the work.

Sometimes you can get double the price of an un-restored and cleaned painting, then the price for a restored work, depending on the quality of the restoration, but in most cases you will get more for a cleaned and restored painting.

Also learning how to do art restoration yourself is an excellent technique and in my travels I have run into many a weekend part time art dealer that does just that. As a matter of fact I personally have restored many paintings myself, one example is a painting that I had acquired that I determined was by a popular contemporary artist from Boston, and it looked like the painting had a slash cut straight through it. The cut was 2 feet long!, I then researched the value and determined it was below Sotheby's price level, around $4500, and decided to restore it myself and place it in a smaller auction house near the Boston area.

I used a very good technique, without having to reline the painting. I used 5 minute epoxy, to glue the cut together, as the cut was a very clean cut. Then I made sure that the glue point was sanded and matched the canvas in the back.

Then I proceeded to use the same medium of paint used by the artist to touch up the line in the front being careful not to over paint the original paint that the artist used, (which would have caused the black light to show the restoration).

When I was finished the painting was fully restored, and the black light showed no restoration. And the contemporary painting which was wonderful was able to be placed in an auction. If I would have gone to a restoration house, this would have cost over $2500 and would have taken a couple of weeks. At any rate the painting was sold for $6500 and the restoration took only an hour or 2 of my time.

This is a great example of a top secret technique that is used by many weekend art dealers quite a bit, and its also very gratifying to do this kind of work, as low end priced art is no longer thrown away, and can be saved and placed for all to see!

AIC is a great place to start to look for an art conservator it's at:

http://www.conservation-us.org

From humble beginnings and a handful of members in 1972, AIC has grown to over 3,500 conservators, educators, scientists, students, archivists, art historians, and other conservation enthusiasts in over twenty countries around the world, all of whom have the same goal: to preserve the material evidence of our past so we can learn from it today and appreciate it in the future.

Also here is another great source:

https://www.art-care.com

Art-Care is an interactive web site designed as a tool to aid art and artifact owners in making informed decisions when selecting a qualified conservator, appraiser, or any other necessary art related service provider.

Top Secret Technique 28
Little known Top Secret, be a self made expert PHD in identifying frames

Antique, gilded picture frames have become very valuable. There was a show, "The Art of the Frame," celebrating a collection of American frames of the Arts and Crafts period, the years from 1870 to 1920. Some of the frames on the walls of this show were priced at $20,000 or more.

Famous artists and crafts- men have historically fashioned frames for art. Each felt they were making a statement in their creations of the frames they made. So this is why they have value like the artworks that are displayed in them. $500 to $800 was a fair price for some frames in the 1980's.

Such a frame was worth as much as $10,000 by mid-1990. During the 1990's only seventeenth and eighteenth century European frames were selling for high amounts in New York. As it is extremely rare for a frames of the 1700's to be found in perfect condition in 2012.

Some sellers restore these frames before they sell them. It is better not to restore the frames, and to keep them as close to their age as possible, not even dusting them off.

Their value will be much higher if they are in good shape and have not been completely restored. Period frames have the best value much higher than reproductions of those period frames. You should be able to identify if a frame is old or a reproduction. Nineteenth-century frames are molded rather than carved, their wood bases covered with a layer of composition material that was then either gilded or painted. Because these frames are prone to decay or can crumble, restoration of these frames has always been difficult, many times often impossible.

Until the 1980s, commercial framers were interested only in selling a frame that was perfect; thus nineteenth-century frames with their flawed surfaces were considered junk, and that idea persisted until their value ultimately came to be recognized. Nobody seemed to care about frames made after 1900, so acquiring them in earlier times was possible.

Today, unique and important frames are increasingly rare. Art dealers feel possessive about their frame acquisitions and auction houses no longer dispose of old frames routinely. Most of the inventory of valuable frames comes from people's attics: frames that have been stored, collected and hidden for years, sometimes many years.

They often find their way into country auctions and tag sales. In the current art market there is a direct correlation between the value of a painting and that of its frame, and as the worth of a painting increases, so does the value of its frame. People who buy a painting in its original frame, or find an important frame to surround a significant purchase, want to look at that painting on the wall in that frame. James McNeill Whistler like many other artists designed his own frames.

A great book on art frames is:

Antique American Frames: Identification and Price Guide Paperback – July 1, 1995 by Eli Wilner (Author), Mervyn Kaufman (Author)

Whether they are elaborately gilded or clean and classic, picture frames are often viewed as works of art. Now there's a fascinating, informative guide to collecting and restoring antique American frames. The book is divided chronologically into design periods, with detailed descriptions of styles and designs.

Examples of Frame sales:

A fine and rare George II giltwood picture
frame in the manner of Thomas Chippendale
mid-18th century
Auction Estimate 30,000 — 50,000 USD
LOT SOLD. 221,000 USD
(Hammer Price with Buyer's Premium)

An Italian carved giltwood frame Venetian, circa 1760
Estimate 4,000 — 6,000 GBP
Lot Sold 5,000 GBP

An Italian 17th Century carved and gilded frame

Lot Sold US$ 2,449

An Italian late 16th Century carved,

ebonised and parcel gilt cassetta frame

Lot Sold US$ 2,974

Also as another example of rare frames discovered Eli Wilner & Company was proud to announce their acquisition of a highly important California Gold Rush-era Jones & Wooll picture frame, circa 1850, gilded with applied ornament in 2015. The frame has a sight size of 29 3/8 X 47 ½ inches with a width of 6 inches. It has an outside measurement of 41 3/8 X 59 ½ inches. This frame is being offered by Eli Wilner & Company for $250,000.

The stenciled name and address on the verso of the frame helped in determining its San Francisco origins. Jones & Wooll were active during the 1850s and 60s and were widely recognized for the quality of their work. Given the city's subsequent history of fires and earthquakes, the fact that this frame has survived in near perfect condition makes it a rare find.

So as an art dealer you have to be on the lookout for not just art but the art of the frame!

Top Secret Technique 29
If it Walks like a Duck, and Talks like a Duck it might be a Duck or Forgery of a Duck!

There are many ways that a weekend art dealer can use to help decide if a work of art is a forgery or if it is a genuine work of art. One way is to know who the original owner is. If a person actually bought a work of art from the artist that created it this is very good provenance. The second rule is the price you are paying for the work of art. If its quite a large sum, you better make sure the art is real. If you are paying very little then you have a 60/40 chance it is real. An example is that the painting might have been sold to someone for a lot of money and then found out it was a forgery.

Then they sell it at their yard sale for very little because they know it's not worth much. The age of the work has multiple aspects to determining it. An example would be a painting that looks like 1800's, in a frame that looks like 1800's, and a stretcher that has a metal brace that is stamped 1806, and nails all around with irregular heads of the 1800's is probably a real 1800's painting. Bronze sculptures, and stone carved marble, alabaster, serpentine, etc. are very expensive to fake so they can be a safe place for purchase. But again if you are paying thousands of dollars, anything can be duplicated.

Top Secret Technique 30
Top Secret Art Dealer Tool the Catalog Raisonne

As we research our artworks we have many tools that help us in determining the authenticity, and value of each item. A biography is a good source or an exhibition catalog of the artist's gallery shows is useful but there is also a possibility that the artist you are researching may have a Catalog Raisonne. The catalog raisonne is a wonderful tool; most artists that have been successful in creating a large amount of artworks have catalog raisonne's published about their careers. A catalog raisonne is usually made up of all the works the artist has done. It helps us understand the years and styles of the artist works. With Fine Art Prints, the Raisonne can help prove that an artist actually did an unsigned work. Also if an artwork you find is signed and the same artwork pictured in the raisonne is not signed it might mean that the work you have has a signature that is a forgery.

Catalog Raisonne's can be very expensive to buy, because there are very few usually created. They are generally compiled by academic professional people and have only a few libraries and art institutions that need them in their collections.

Some Catalog Raisonne's can be $10,000 for each book. Because of this most people will access the raisonne at the larger main libraries, colleges, and museum libraries. If you have an artwork by an artist, it is sometimes beneficial to have that artwork included in a Catalogue Raisonne. I was amazed to find that if you type "Catalogue Raisonne" in the search of google.com you get tons of people looking for proven works by artists for catalogue raisonne compilations. In the Art Signature File CD-Rom there is a complete list of resources for finding artists Catalogue Raisonne and research tips.

Especially for art prints of the 20th and the 19th century, documentations were made by scholars, publishers, art enthusiasts and sometimes by the artists themselves about all the works created by a particular artist. These documentations describing each work painstakingly with all details, are called a catalog raisonne.

From Wikipedia:

https://en.wikipedia.org/wiki/Catalogue_raisonn%C3%A9

A catalogue raisonné is a comprehensive, annotated listing of all the known artworks by an artist either in a particular medium or all media.[1] The works are described in such a way that they may be reliably identified by third parties.

There are many variations, both broader and narrower than "all the works" or "one artist". The parameters may be restricted to one type of art work by one artist or widened to all the works by a group of artists. It can take many years to complete a catalogue raisonné and large teams of researchers are sometimes employed on the task.

For example, it was reported in 2013 that the Dedalus Foundation (established by the abstract-expressionist painter Robert Motherwell) took 11 years to complete the three-volume catalogue raisonné of Motherwell's work which was published by Yale University Press in 2012, with approximately 25 people contributing to the project.

Advice on How to research with Catalogue Raisonne From the New York Public Library

"What is a Catalogue Raisonné?

A catalogue raisonné is a comprehensive, annotated listing of all the known works of an artist either in a particular medium or all media. They may provide some or all of the following:

Title and title variations

Dimension/Size

Date of the work

Medium

Current location/owner at time of publication

Provenance (history of ownership)

Exhibition history

Condition of the work

Bibliography/Literature that discusses the work

Essay(s) on the artist

Critical assessments and remarks

Full description of the work

Signatures, Inscriptions, and Monograms of the artist

Reproduction of each work

List of works attributed, lost, destroyed, and fakes

Catalog number

However, not all raisonnés are identified in the Catalog; some may be listed under the subject: 'Catalogs.'

Other terms that may be used in place of catalogue raisonné are:

Oeuvre

Catalogo Razonado

Catalogo Ragionato

Catalogo Generale

Opera Completa

Werkverzeichnis

Leben und Werk

Oeuvrekatalog

Complete Works

Critical Catalogue

Life and Work

The catalogue raisonnés collection is located and requested at the reference desk in the Art & Architecture Collection; the call numbers begin with (C.R.).

According to some scholars, not all volumes collected and placed in our reference desk collection are true catalogues raisonnés.

We have included books that provide the closest listing of all the works of an artist that is available at the moment. Any raisonnés dealing with etchings, lithographs, and prints are housed in our Print Collection, Room 308.

Organizations Dealing with Catalogues raisonné:
Catalogue Raisonné Scholars Association
International Foundation for Art Research (IFAR)
Index to Print Catalogues Raisonnés:
The Print Council Index to Oeuvre-Catalogues of Prints by European and American Artists

So as you research always remember to see if there is a Catalogue Raisonne available for the artist you are researching. In the Raisonne, you might just see the work of art that you have discovered, and that would be the ultimate provenance when you go to market your artworks!

Top Secret Technique 31
Every time you place a work of Art you might be making history!

When the weekend art dealer discovers a work of art he or she becomes a part of that artworks history. It's a simple concept, the art is discovered and then it begins the identification and marketing process.

When the art is sold it usually goes to a collector or gallery, or museum. This is where it is placed for future generations to see it or study it. I knew a dealer who had a work of art he discovered in a dumpster, the work of art was finally placed and sold for a nice profit.

The work turned out to be a sketch or study for a greater much larger important work of art by a famous artist. The artist was part of a short lived movement and very little was known about the development of his techniques during this period. This work of art helped fill in the blank areas, and was historically very important to the scholars who were studying these artists' techniques.

Another kind of placement of art is through Public Art programs. Public art is usually installed with the authorization and collaboration of the government or company that owns or administers the space. Some governments actively encourage the creation of public art, for example, budgeting for artworks in new buildings by implementing a Percent for Art policy. 1% of the construction cost for art is a standard, but the amount varies widely from place to place.

The first percent-for-art legislation passed in Philadelphia in 1959. This requirement is implemented in a variety of ways. The government of Quebec maintains the art and architecture integration policy requiring the budget for all new publicly funded buildings set aside approximately 1% for artwork.

New York City has a law that requires that no less than 1% of the first twenty million dollars, plus no less than one half of 1% of the amount exceeding twenty million dollars be allocated for art work in any public building that is owned by the city. The maximum allocation for any commission in New York is.

More information on Public Art Placement can be seen here:

Forecast Public Art has created an on line "toolkit" to learn the basics of the public art field. It is free to use, and although it was created for the Minnesota context it can be used by anyone. http://forecastpublicart.org/toolkit/

By Placing art in galleries, collections, museums, or in Public Art programs, You will be making history, every time you do a transaction for placing an art work. This has happened many times and undiscovered works are being found more often than not, so make some history this weekend and get out there and place a work of art and earn something!

Top Secret Technique 32
Places for Art Discovery

Its amazing some of the best places to discover art includes Basements, Attics, Garages, Storage Rooms, Barns, Laying on piles of garbage, Dumpsters, Estate sales, Yard sales, Garage sales, Flea markets, Thrift sales, Church sales, Rummage sales, Metal recycling companies, On the wall of a friend, On the wall of a family member, Museum De-Accessions, Public Administrator Auctions, Ebay, Yahoo, and about 200 other not so well publicized online auctions.

Also Tias is a great place for Art Discoveries:

http://www.tias.com/art

Artspace.com sell work from top artists, both established (like Eric Fischl, Sally Mann, and Chuck Close) and little known, without the gallery markup. Prices start at $100.

Go Lateral,

as Art Can Be Discovered Anywhere!
Place an Ad, Email and Ask People!

Jan Johnson Prints carries

old master prints:

Artists they carry are:

OLD MASTER

BEHAM, Hans Sebald and Barthel

BELLA, Stefano della

BONASONE, Giulio

BRUEGHEL, Pieter the Elder, after

CALLOT, Jacques

CANALETTO, Antonio Canal, called

CASTIGLIONE, Giovanni Benedetto

COCK, Hieronymus

DURER, Albrecht

FRYE, Thomas

GELLÉE, Claude, called Le Lorrain

GHEYN, Jacob de, II and III

GOLTZIUS, Hendrick

HEEMSKERCK, Maerten van, by & after

MULLER, Jan

NANTEUIL, Robert

OSTADE, Adriaen van

PIRANESI, Giovanni Battista

REMBRANDT van Rijn

ROSA, Salvator

SADELER, Aegidius and Jan

SAENREDAM, Jan

SWANEVELT, Herman van

TESTA, Pietro

TIEPOLO, Giambattista and Giandomenico

VELDE, Esais and Jan van de

WATERLOO, Anthonie

MODERN

BECKMANN, Max

BESNARD, Albert

BLAKE, William

BONNARD, Pierre

BRESDIN, Rodolphe

BROCKHURST, Gerald

BUHOT, Felix

CHAHINE, Edgar

DAUMIER, Honoré

GOYA, Francisco

GRIGGS, Frederick

GROS, Baron

HADEN, Sir Frances Seymour

IBELS, Henri-Gabriel

ISABEY, Eugenen

KLINGER, Max

KOLBE, Karl Wilhelm

MARTIN, John

MERYON, Charles

PISSARRO, Camille

RANFT, Richard

TISSOT, Jacques

VALLOTTON, Felix

VILLON, Jacques

VLAMINCK, Maurice de

VUILLARD, Edouard

WHISTLER, James McNeill

CANADIAN

BIELER, André

GAGNON, Clarence

GORANSON, Paul

HOLGATE, Edwin

NEILSON, Henry Ivan

PHILLIPS, W.J.

RAINE, Herbert

In the back of this book I have a listing area for places to search for art to buy, auction art and places to sell art, and also there are great places you can research your art.

I have tried to be as comprehensive as possible so that you can be successful in your art research adventures.

Also it is important to know that anywhere antiques are sold (flea markets, antique shows, dealer stores) are a great place to discover art, I have found many modern works of art using this technique!

Pop Art Artists and some prices...

Adami, Valerio $17,000

Amen, Woody van $750

Arman $365,000

Artschwager, Richard $65,000

Asselbergs, Gustave $9500

Baldaccini, Cesar $60,000

Barker, Clive $2500

Bentum, Rik van $3500

Blake, Peter $20,000

Boshier, Derek $7500

Boty, Pauline

Caulfield, Patrick $20,000

d'Arcangelo, Allan $20,000

de-Guillebon, Jeanne-Claude

Dine, Jim $250,000

Donaldson, Antony $2000

Escobar, Marisol $65,000

Fahlstrom, Oyvind $100,000

Hains, Raymond $20,000

Hamilton, Richard $40,000

Hockney, David $5,407,407

Hopper, Dennis $165,282

Top Secret Technique 33 Techniques used for looking at the pricing structure of Art from the near past to the present

The near past prices of art pretty much set the current price a work of art should sell for. The factors are:

1. The perception of the art world – art historians, critics, collectors, gallery experts helps determine pricing.

2. History or provenance can determine the value of a work of art; Provenance is the history of ownership of a work of art. Who owned the work of art can add to the value of that work of art. Any documentation of the ownership of the art work shows that the piece is authentic, original and not a reproduction or a forgery, or that it is a stolen work of art.

3. Also the provenance of a work of art might be included in a catalogue raisonné or in other writings by the artist, letters or details in archives of art. Establishing the provenance of a work of fine art is important to know where it came from, how it was acquired and who owned it previously to help in determining its market price.

4. The importance of an artist as an influence on his generation is a factor, amounts of artworks done if there are relatively few pieces, and if the artist has works that are mostly are in museum collections.

5. Then you have to write down all these possible things you can get about the work of art:

a. Title or subject matter of the art

b. Name of the artist

c. Date or approximate age of the art

d. Edition size and number

e. If it is a print or graphic

f. Medium (oil painting, watercolor,

Drawing print sculpture, collage etc):

g. Measurements and Condition

h. Ownership history or provenance

i. Locate and Markings, or Text of any

Stickers, stamps, or labels on the art

j. Where was it purchased (Sothebys?

Christies? or other

k. How much was it purchased for?

l. Do you know the Importance of the artist?

m. Does the work of art have a frame?

n. Is it the original frame? Always identify the frame.

6. Then examine the work, take measurements, notes about condition, signature, any other physical traits.

7. Then take a photograph of the art object.

8. Looking at the back of two-dimensional works is as important as looking at the front since there are often gallery stickers or identifying features which are extremely useful in determining provenance.

9. Art appraisers are experts in examining and researching an art work and its provenance, so if you discover a document attached to the back of the artwork this can help in evaluating the price.

10. You should not remove an old picture from it's frame, or clean a frame as this can lower the price of the work of art, and some buyers like having the work of art in original condition when they purchase art.

11. Clean the glass, if it has glass then use a magnifying glass to look at the picture in greater detail for age, and signature evaluation.

12. In some cases limited edition prints by a well-known artists, have a greater value than a genuine painting by an unknown artist.

13. In all cases retain the original frame as sometimes frames can fetch higher prices than the actual art work.

14. Examine with a black light, also referred to as a UV light, ultraviolet light, or Wood's lamp and do infrared reflectography on the artwork, this can give information about repairs, restorations, fake signatures, and under

painting, which can help determine the value of the work of art.

15. In the end you can also get a general value of a work of art using standard art dealer practices and a price guide like The Art Signature File, that has signatures, of artists matched to their average sales records at auction, to get the approximate value, and then sell it.

Determining the price of art from past provenance is an analysis of how effectively the artist is promoted to all aspects of the art world. The more effectively an artists works have been promoted to galleries determines, museum curators and the collectors buying decisions. If the artist or gallery really promotes artworks the demand will be created for their work and higher prices can be achieved. Example: Thomas Kinkade to most people he was not that good of an artist, but he was very good at public relations. Kinkade produced around $100 million a year selling originals and reproductions. William Thomas Kinkade III (January 19, 1958 – April 6, 2012) was an American painter of popular realistic, pastoral, and idyllic subjects. He is notable for the mass marketing of his work as printed reproductions and other licensed products via the Thomas Kinkade Company. His prints can sell from $150 to $375 and an original painting of his just sold for $150,000!

Top Secret Technique 34
Find at least one work of art every week that you know you can sell

To be a successful part time week end art dealer, you do not only have to have selling channels set up so you have places and methods to sell. But you need to have ways and channels for acquiring artworks every week.

One top secret technique is to set up connections with contemporary artists that will give you some of their art to try to market. Another technique is that on the weekend go to as many sales as you can as an adventure, and try to make it a habit to find at least one work of art at a reasonable price that you know you can sell for a profit.

Some very good places that are open every weekend are flea markets, thrift stores, and yard sales garage sales, and other areas that have used goods for sale.

Also maybe you have an artist in the family, so you can make a deal with your aspiring relative or friend, that they create for you works of art that you can market and sell for them at a commission, during your dry periods where you can not find art.

You can also as you go along give the aspiring artist recommendations as you will be in the selling area of art dealing and you will know what sells and what does not. At any rate this process will keep you focused on the real work of being an art dealer, and if you can sell a new artists works then you can sell anything.

When you look at artworks out there, always look at it from what you think the art can be sold for. Of course first check out the signature, and the style, and the age, etc. But you can make profits as a market sale if you believe the value of the artwork.

You have to believe what it is worth, sometimes by just the value of what some work of art has sold for before as a comparison.

So it would go like this:

A. Art work size is 12 x14 inches

B. It's a watercolor

C. It looks like a landscape

D. The age is from the 1920's

E. It's well painted

F. You can not determine who the artist is

G. Nice Frame

So you would say that you would pay $20 low end price, and that you could sell it for $45. Get this embedded in your brain. Then go to the person selling the art, ask them what would they take? They say $50 or $5 you never know... If they say $50 you say will you take $20? If not you walk away... Or you find 3 other works of art and offer them $60 for all 3 works of art. As an Art Dealer you need to resell your purchases well!

Top Secret Technique 35
The Yard Sale "Auction", and
How to prevent it

Sometimes when you are out shopping at yard sales, garage sales or in public places where other shoppers are around you, you discover a great work of art. Then as you proceed to ask how much the work of art is from the person running the sale, there is sometimes another customer, looking over your shoulder, and they have an interest in the art also, and after the price is stated, you have the opportunity to buy, but the other customer says that he will pay more for the art.

And this is what is called a "yard sale auction", even though there is no auction at that sale. The way to get around this very bad situation is to always try to be private in your pricing requests, and be aware of other customers hovering around you as you view art items at sales.

One example of how these spontaneous "yard sale auctions" can create a bad situation is the fact that when a seller gives you a price you should have the ability to counter offer on the price, and maybe get a better price, if the price seems too high.

If another customer or two start showing interest then it's difficult to get a better price and you might even have to pay a much higher price than the original price that the seller wanted to get. Also remember to get the money into the hand of the seller, after the price is set as soon as you can, and remove the item from view of other buyers. And never go to a cash machine and come back because another buyer might negotiate a sale while you are gone.

One last thing I ran into in my adventures was that if I went to a local sale and anyone knew I was walking around shopping they would sometimes follow me to see what I picked up, and would hover around, knowing that I was an expert in art, hoping to get a valuable work of art that I put down for a moment.

This technique works very well for a lot of art collectors and dealers that have very little imagination and knowledge. You see things that do not interest anyone at sales, become very interesting once a person starts to look at it. It is called "perceived value". Everyone likes to get things that other people want, so anything that has anyone interested creates a market curiosity in the item, and the perceived value moves upward in price in the mind of the people observing other people taking an interest in a work of art.

The worst aspect of this is when people know you are a well known art dealer, then they all know you would not be looking at something unless it is a very good work of art. I used to have many people who would follow me around looking at what I picked up, and then when I briefly put the art down, they ran and scooped it up, this is a true story!

Top Secret Technique 36 Researching the Artist for Clues about Art

Sometimes when doing research on art we run in to elements of the work of art that lead us to discover important information about places, styles, and techniques of art at the time of creation that can help add an interesting story to the art.

A good example of this technique, is that once while on a weekend excursion in New York City a friend and I came upon a work of art that had what looked like melted crayons, that from close up looked very abstract, and when you looked further out at a distance the work of art showed 1940's cars and what looked like a Broadway theatre in the background, and it looked like the paintings perspective viewpoint was from the 2nd or 3rd floor of a building, across from a Broadway theatre. On the back of the work of art it had in pen, "for Rob to bring".

So the first thing that we did was to identify who in the 1940's was located right across from the Broadway musical Oklahoma as the work of art had that painted on the billboard over the theatre.

We came up with a history of Jasper Johns and Robert Raushenberg that they both lived together after world war two around 1948 when the musical Oklahoma was first playing on

Broadway. Next we determined that the "johns for rob to bring" might mean Jasper Johns and he might have wrote this as something that was to be brought to an exhibition, as they exhibited together at that time. Also it was determined that Jasper Johns also worked in encaustic painting, hot wax like the melted crayon used in this painting. We also found out that the earlier works of Jasper Johns were destroyed by the artist, in a fire when he got frustrated with the art he was doing and he changed his style completely after that time.

Was this a lost work of art by the famous Jasper Johns? Only time will tell as further research is needed to provide the, facts and information for a positive conclusion. This is what art research is about and its like a Sherlock Holmes investigation, and when the results lead to positive identification that is a great feeling knowing that an artwork has been placed for the future art viewer to see.

Sometimes the artist's life can define the work of art, as many artists paint their surroundings, their journey, or just the people that they have met in their life. So if you know the artist, and their life, the art can be identified beyond a shadow of a doubt using this technique.

This is the process of simple deduction in the art research process, and it works very well for most weekend art dealers. Also sometimes a seller will tell a story of the artist as you are trying to determine the value of art. This can give you a lot to work with, as unknown artists sometimes are very relevant!

Top Secret Technique 37
Decorate with Investment grade Fine Art Works

One of the best ways to build an art gallery for a weekend art dealer is to decorate your home with investment grade works of art. That way if someone is over for a visit and is interested in buying art, they can see it at your home gallery, and purchase it. Also at any time it is good to tell your friends and people you meet that they should also decorate with fine artwork, as one can enjoy the works of art, and as the years go by they will appreciate in value if they are works by desirable artists.

Almost every office of successful people has works of art that are considered investment grade art. In history there have been many acquisitions made by major corporations for the lobbies of their buildings. Also some of the wealthiest people in the world have great art collections. This practice is not a new one as many art galleries began in people's homes, the Barnes collection in Philadelphia, is a great example, and Sotheby's periodically has sales from collections that were in home galleries of famous collectors.

I remember even my great grandfather had an art gallery in his house, during the late 1800's. Of course at that time pastures with cows and beautiful angelic scenes were popular, works of art that were exhibited on those walls.

Top Secret Technique 38
Collecting is inevitable with the true Art Dealer!

Collecting art is inevitable as you pursue your weekend art dealer adventure. Sometimes you will find a sale where you can pick up a whole collection of art works for a very reasonable price. When this happens you may see some works that you want to keep for yourself.

It's not unusual for an art dealer to keep the best for themselves, and sell only the works of art that the art dealer collector does not want. By being a weekend part time art dealer, you are not giving up your main job and so it's easier to hold on to the quality works of art for your own collection.

Artist Prices...

Indiana, Robert $500,000

Jeong-Hwa, Choi

Johns, Jasper $80,000,000

Jones, Allen

Kanovitz, Howard $14,000

Kaufman, Steve

Kienholz, Edward $17,000

Kitaj, R B $3,000,000

Top Secret Technique 39 Letters at an Artist estate can be Enlightening Treasures!

If you ever stumble upon an artists, art collector, gallery owner, or art academic estate sale, you should be very attentive at looking at the letters, receipts, writings, correspondence, paper items like gallery show catalogues, brochures, drawings and anything art related.

By looking at these often overlooked items you sometimes can get very important historical data related to the relationships, and friendships between artists and art collectors, curators, galleries, and the techniques of art business in general.

Most people at these sales overlook these important documents. A lot of times the documents are donated to the Archives of American Art, Smithsonian, or other international museum archives, for use in future art research. And you can actually view these documents at those locations.

But many times I have been to a sale where the family of the art related person, just did not know the importance of the letters, photos, and catalogues, and they just planned to throw them out because they wanted to sell the house.

I remember a time where works or art, and all the letters receipts and photos related to a very significant illustrator collector from the 1900's was discovered in a dumpster. And the some of the works found in that dumpster were sold for over $80,000.

But the main research aspects of this discovery was that the actual receipts for the artworks that were found were there lying next to them in that dumpster. The receipts gave a very important clue into where the works of art were purchased, and this led to many discoveries there.

But by the time that a lot of the works were researched, that dumpster had been picked up and the works were discarded. Since that time I always try to rescue all works of art that are discovered in the trash, as this was very disturbing. I hope that the works of art were pulled out at the city dump, but probably not.

Some artist prices...

Richter, Gerhard $2,000,000

Rivers, Larry $450,000

Rosenquist, James $300,000

Ruscha, Edward $3,000,000

Scharf, Kenny $7000

Segal, George $600,000

Self, Colin $1500

Smith, Richard $12,000

Thiebaud, Wayne $500,000

Tilson, Joe $8000

Warhol, Andy $71,700,000

Top Secret Technique 40
How to tell the Date of a work of Art

Physical evidence often reliably indicates an object's age. The material used for the creation by the artist of a statue, painting, sculpture, print, drawing, bronze, plastic, or oil-based pigment, may not have been invented before a certain time, indicating the earliest possible date someone could have created the work of art.

Also artists may have stopped using certain materials, such as specific kinds of inks and papers for drawings and prints at a documented time, providing the latest possible dates for works of art made of such materials. Sometimes the material or the creation technique of a work of art can establish a very precise date of creation of the work of art.

Documentary evidence also can help focus in on the date of work of art when a dated written document mentions the work. Visual evidence plays a significant role in dating an artwork. An artist might have depicted an identifiable person or a kind of hairstyle, clothing, or furniture fashionable only at a certain time.

If so, the art researcher can determine an approximate date to that work of art. Stylistic evidence is also very important. The analysis of an artworks style is an artist's distinctive manner of creating an artwork. Stylistic evidence is by far the most unreliable way to date a work of art. Still, art dealers find style a very useful tool for establishing the date of an artwork as styles, were established in a certain timeframe and are documented. In the back of this book there are many styles and dates of when they were prevalent.

Impressionism

Impressionism movement was started in France during the mid 1860s and throughout the 1870s. The principle Impressionist painters were Pierre Auguste Renoir, Claude Monet, Paul Cézanne, Camille Pissarro, Alfred Sisley and Berthe Morisot, and Edgar Degas.

The French Impressionists

Frederic Bazille $500,000

Eugene Boudin $1,600,000

Felix Bracquemond $10,000

Marie Bracquemond $7500

Mary Cassatt $4,072,500

Gustave Caillebotte $14,300,000

Paul Cezanne $60,500,000

Gustave Colin $4700

Edgar Degas $28,000,000

Top Secret Technique 41
Art Research on works on paper is like Sherlock Holmes, Simple Deduction Watson!

In purchasing art works the art dealer has to have an idea of what is being bought. As far as art works on paper we have to ask these questions, during our art research, and acquisitions:

1. Is it a drawing created in charcoal? ink? or pencil? or another technique?
2. Is it an aquatint? Is it a watercolor? Is it a gouache?
3. Is it an example of multiple printing techniques like etching with drypoint?
4. Is this a print at all? Is it a lithograph? a serigraph? an etching? an engraving? a monotype? a collotype? a poster? a giclee? or a magazine reproduction?
5. What does the mat and frame look like? What type of condition are they in? Are they damaged?
6. Where the mat was cut, does it look yellow or brown in color?
7. Is the entire work on paper sort of brown or beige, too? If so non acid free mounting might be at work

on the work of art, and should be taken in to account in the costs for restoration.

8.   Check for Foxing which looks like little specs of dark brown in areas on the work of art; most prevalent and easy to recognize on works on paper. Foxing can be corrected, but it will increase the cost of the restoration of the work of art on paper subtracted from your bottom line profit.

Dada

Dada can be traced to the Cabaret Voltaire in Zurich in 1916, and another group was quickly organized in New York by Marcel Duchamp, movement centered at Gallery 291. The leading spirit of Dada was Marcel Duchamp.

Dada artists

Arp, Hans $450,000
Baader, Johannes $60,000
Baargeld, Johannes Theodor $30,000
Blumenfeld, Erwin $3000

Top Secret Technique 42
You can Make $1000 or even $100,000 extra cash, as a part time Art Dealer!

Most of the part time art dealers that I know of earn at least $3000 to $5000 a month extra in their endeavors. But you can make as little as $1000 if you do not work at it, but I have known week end art dealers that have averaged $100,000 a month!

It's all how you manage your time and set up your network of sales points. It is always very important to have a network of other dealers, galleries, auction houses, and places to sell art, so that from every weekend art adventure, you are making some sales. Whether it is online, offline in flea markets, direct sales to dealers and collectors, you need a network of ways to move and churn your sales.

This should be one of the first things you should set up in your weekend art dealer's brokerage after you buy your first artworks. In this process you will be taught quickly what the other dealers, collectors auctions, galleries will buy from you, and what sells best online!

Some Dada Artists

Drier, Katherine Sophie $2500

Duchamp, Marcel $1,762,500

Eggeling, Viking $30,000

Ernst, Max $2,429,500

Freytag-Loringhoven, Baroness Elsa von

Golyscheff, Jefim $23,000

Grosz, George $150,000

Hausmann, Raoul $400,000

Heartfield, John $3500

Hoch, Hannah $824,000

Huelsenbeck, Richard $1000

Janco, Marcel $40,000

Man Ray $1,504,440

Picabia, Francis $4,780,880

Prampolini, Enrico $85,000

Richter, Hans $30,000

Schad, Christian $200,000

Schamberg, Morton Livingston
$280,000

Schwitters, Kurt $170,000

Stieglitz, Alfred $100,000

Taeuber-Arp, Sophie $65,000

Tschichold, Jan $1500

Van Doesburg, Theo $200,000

Top Secret Technique 43
The Gypsy Harvest Ball every October!

In October every year in my territory all the dealers had a favorite event, it was called the Gypsy Harvest Ball, and it was the time of the year that a certain affluent neighborhood would clean out their attics, basements, and garages of things they did not want for the year to come.

All the antique and art dealers that attended, came home with some great things, some contemporary works of art, photos, antique paintings, frames from the Hudson river period, and many collectible items. All of this was free to take and made for interesting art research.

There are many of these all over the USA and in many international areas. The good thing about this particular one was that while you were driving around in those areas, looking for treasures, on the streets, some people had garage sales and yard sales as a group event.

Imagine being able to get free items and buy great works of art at the sales from the community!

Abstract Expressionism

The founders of Abstract Expressionism include Hans Hofmann, Willem de Kooning, Arshile Gorky, Jackson Pollock, Mark Rothko, and Franz Kline.

Some Abstract Expressionism artists

Baziotes, William $300,000

Bluhm, Norman $47,000

Davie, Alan $42,000

Firestone, Robert

Francis, Sam $4,048,000

Frankenthaler, Helen $800,000

Gambini, William

Goldberg, Michael $25,000

Gorky, Arshile $3,962,500

Guston, Philip $1,835,500,000

Hartigan, Grace $10,000

Hofmann, Hans $4,297,000

Kline, Franz $6,400,000

Kooning, Elaine de $1,142,500

Kooning, Willem de $63,500,000

Krasner, Lee $3,170,000

Mitchell, Joan $9,300,000

Top Secret Technique 44 Flashlight People in Mink Coats!

Flea Markets are great places to find a concentration of works of art, what is good about flea markets is that they are usually new things discovered from the week before, so the artwork gets churned every week. The reason is that if you do not have new things to sell every week, you will not make any money selling in these markets. So every week you can have different things to choose from.

Some of the dealers at the flea markets are not so sophisticated, and they just want to move the items, so they sometimes do not have the time to research the works of art. In the early 70's there were recessions that led to the flea markets sprouting up and even into today there are many all over the world. There is a famous flea market in New York City the 26th street flea market. It was an amazing flea market as dealers would pull up in their vans on Saturday and Sunday and unload their acquisitions from the week before at 4 am in the morning. It so happens that I tried it a couple of times, and it was amazing, at 4 am when the vans pulled in, the flea market dealers would start unloading, and the buyers in mink coats, and professional buyers with flash lights would be all over the place.

They would be the first to see what was being setup, and many huge deals were completely transacted by 5 am on those mornings. Some of these wealthy buyers were film producers, directors, writers, famous artists, bankers, art dealers, executives, wealthy housewives, and others. They were all there to see the art before anyone else. There were million dollar works of art discovered there that way in the past. It was an exciting thing to see. Sometimes there would be bidding wars that would happen between a mink coat lady and an executive banker over a work of art, all to the benefit of the flea market seller. But most of the time these affluent buyers would respect the common courtesy rules of engagement in buying at these flea markets.

It would be something to see these well dressed people with flashlight, buying things they could barely see, but no one wanted to leave a potential new addition to their collections to any of the other group of buyers. By 7 am the other early bird buyers started to show up with the light of day and whatever was left was still very impressive, and I have known many people who have found many valuable works of art, sculpture, or works on paper all day long at that market. But understand very clearly there are unlimited amounts of works of art to be found, and placed all over the country. In small towns there are flea markets and you would be surprised at what you can find if you are smart and know what to look for.

One man's trash is another's treasure and believe me there are treasures out there. In the most difficult of time these days this is the grass roots way of keeping a float in difficult times. As a weekend art dealer, you can get exciting and adventurous ways to supplement your income, and learn about people and their works of art they created, so it is a win win accomplishment.

Futurism

Futurism was developed in Italy around 1900. The main members of the Futurists included Carlo Carrà and Umberto Boccioni.

Some of The Futurist's artists

Acquaviva, Giovanni $1000

Azari, Fedele

Baldessari, Iras $30,000

Baldessari, Luciano $3000

Balla, Giacomo $4,400,000

Barbieri, Osvaldo

Boccioni, Umberto $600,000

Bragaglia, Carlo

Bragaglia, Anton

Burliuk, David $55,000

L. Emile Adan

LOUIS EMILE ADAN 1839-1937
French, Genre, Landscape $15,000

Adler

JANKEL ADLER 1895-1949
Polish Painter, Portraits, Nudes $100,000

S.M. Adler

SAMUEL ADLER 1898-1979
American Modern $1,000

Edmund Adler

EDMUND ADLER 1871-1957
Austrian Painter $10,000

Andreenko

MIKHAIL ADREENKO 1894-1982
Russian Painter $5,000

Lucien Adrion

LUCIEN ADRION 1889-1953
French Painter $20,000

10

Top Secret Technique 45
How to display Art for
Maximum profits!

I have found that art can be displayed in many ways for maximum profits in your home gallery, gallery or at a show, or flea market booth. You should always show your art in its best light, so that the beauty of the art comes out. Also always hang the art in a pleasant way for viewing as this makes it easy for the potential buyer to see it and imagine it in their possession. But another top secret technique used by many weekend art dealers is the stacking of works of art down against a wall or support, so it looks like no one has viewed them before. Potential buyers in flea markets like to think they have found something, that they only were the only one to discover.

Of course in your home gallery or outside gallery the prices will be much higher, and the works of art have to be in good condition and ready to take home and add to the buyer's collection. Remember, good lighting, is important, and its ok for lots of dust to be on the flea market works of art you display, and clean and not so much dust on your home gallery, or outside gallery works of art.

But uncleaned frames and works of art should be available for those special just acquired viewings in your home gallery or outside gallery, because even the high end buyer of art wants to be the first to see a work of art. And also the value sometimes can be higher for untouched discovered works of art as the buyers sometimes have their own restoration services and people they would prefer to use for the restoration and cleaning.

More Futurists

Cangiullo, Francesco $28,000

Cappa, Benedetta

Carra, Carlo $350,000

Depero, Fortunato $55,000

Dottori, Gerardo $35,000

Goncharova, Natalia $10,870,500

Khlebnikov, Velimir

Kruchenykh, Alexei

Marinetti, Filippo Tommaso $15000

Matiushin, Mikhail $1500

Mayakovski, Vladimir

Munari, Bruno $5000

Popova, Liubov $1,600,000

Prampolini, Enrico $85,000

Russolo, Luigi $420,000

Sassu, Aligi $75,000

Severini, Gino $3,300,000

Sironi, Mario $450,000

Soffici, Ardengo $55,000

Wulz, Wanda

Top Secret Technique 46
Attend often, every month local antique auctions!

The greatest auctions are antique auctions, and estate auctions. These are held every month, and you might have to drive far to get to them but it is worthwhile. These auctions are for clearance of antiques, memorabilia, and art.

You can get great bargains at these auctions and it's a fun outing for your family, friends or art dealer colleagues that might attend with you. Always be careful to note who is working with the auction house trying to bid things up, so that you do not bid things up too high against them.

Also if your friends are bidding make sure you discuss with them what they are buying so you do not bid their prices up and they do not bid on your things.

It's amazing how 3 art dealers can be interested in different kinds of art. I remember one of these auctions once where some Andy Warhol items came up and there were absolutely no bidders interested, but me and some other colleagues that were there. We agreed not to bid against each other but we would split the sale 3 ways at the end.

We were able to get the limited edition serigraphs for very little, as there were no bidders that wanted contemporary works. Afterward the serigraphs, had to be researched, and a trip to the actual serigrapher proved enlightening, they were sold very well privately, and all involved had a nice profit, at the end of the day!

Top Secret Technique 47
Blind fold me, Take me to any town, and I will find a valuable work of art in a short time over the weekend!

I was once traveling to the southern USA and I was in a small town, and was visiting some people there. I wondered, if I could discover a work of art that would be valuable even in this small town, so on one of my excursions I visited a small local indoor flea market and there I wandered through all the booths looking for the elusive treasure I was searching for. As I was with friends I said I bet by the end of the day I will find a work of art that will be very valuable. They were very skeptical so I proceeded to walk around the market, and there were all kinds of antiques, bric a brac, and lamps.

Then I stumbled upon a Coca Cola print or at least it looked like a print. It was hanging up on the wall in the back of a booth. I moved in closer and it was a beautiful original painting, very well done of a blond girl drinking a Coca Cola. So I identified the quality, and immediately asked the proprietor how much was the picture? He responded that it was $30. I could not imagine an original illustration signed and dated 1941, and that was so perfectly painted, was only $30, so I bought it and left the place, when I later researched it, I found out that the illustrator lived in that small town, and was one of the illustrators that was a regular contributor to Coca Cola's advertising campaigns.

I used 2 techniques of the art dealer's top secret techniques of buying art one was to identify value by looking at how the art is painted. The second was to evaluate that if a Coca Cola printed tray can go for between $75 and $150 then what would an illustration be worth? In my head I said well maybe $300. So my decision was set, and I later sold that illustration for $6500 and today some go for as much as $10,000.

It's always good to use some logical collectible instincts when dealing in art!

Top Secret Technique 48
How to set up your Art dealer network

An art dealer network is a simple thing to setup, but it does require you to be an outgoing person. If you are not an outgoing person then go out of your way to become friends with local antique dealers, and through them you will be able to get closer to the art buyers and sellers. They all know who is a specialist in art, and they in turn will assist you in the beginning by helping you sell your art. But remember they will not pay as much as the main art buyers and sellers, as they are a middle person in the process.

Many antique dealers sell art on the side, and they are always looking for art to display in their markets, or stores. Also do not be afraid to try to make deals for splitting anything over a set amount that the art is sold for. Sometimes antique dealers take art on consignment, in other words, they do not buy your art outright, but take it into their store and try to sell it. And when the art is sold they split the sale with you in some way. All of this can be negotiated.

These connections are your art dealer network. In this network there are lower fish in the chain, they are called pickers, these are people who will sometimes find or discover a work of art but are not familiar with identification of art.

Also they pay really low process or find the artworks thrown out. You should encourage these people to bring the art to you first so you can evaluate it, and be generous in any wins that you discover because of these peoples efforts. Pay them well and they will keep looking for you, also give them some advanced money and ask them that if they ever see a work of art at a sale that is interesting stay with it and call you, as every art dealer cannot be at 2 sales at the same time, this can be an invaluable asset to your art dealer network.

Top Secret Technique 49
Be aware of other treasures besides Art

Be aware that there are other things that are valuable also other than art, I mentioned that frames have a value separately, but there are other collectibles and antiques and even things like photographs, and vernacular photographs that are valuable also. An art dealer can sometimes use these items in trades for art with antique dealers, and to sell straight out. Go through the antique dealers stores and look at the prices that the dealer is asking for things, then mention if you ever see an item like that what would you pay me for that? By doing this you have a mental mapping of what you might be able to get for things you see in your adventures.

And also if there is a painting that you want from another dealer, you can sometimes sweeten the deal with some antiques that you will throw into the deal. But also be on the lookout for things like valuable collectible baseball cards like the Honus Wagner tobacco base ball card, which is worth over 1 million dollars, you never know!

Top Secret Technique 50
How to set up your Home or Office Art Dealer Reference library

Your art library is very important to your art dealer business. It should have many books related to styles, price guides, and signature sample books, like The Art Signature File, art books should be more heavily weighted on modern art as related to art from the 1900's on to today. You should also have many Chinese, and Japanese art books, as these are a new frontier in art collecting. Especially wood block prints, and calligraphy art.

You should have not just a historical art section, but a realistic art area with files for current sales prices and photos of art that is selling at auction. This should be where all the art at auction catalogs are located. The best thing for a dealer in art is having the library and files with knowledge of what things have sold for in the past and what they sell for today. Also gallery show catalogs where you have visited, with prices for the many contemporary, and traditional artists and current prices for the artists they represent is useful also. The more you know about what you are dealing in the better your business will run. Also the more organized your art library is the easier and faster you can get results from your research.

Top Secret Technique 51
Auction estimates and reality of price

Estimates are great but sometimes the reality of the price that is hammered down at auction might be totally different. To give you an example once there was this work of art, and it was estimated at a very well known and respectable auction house to sell between $10,000 and $12,000. And on the day of the sale I was in the audience and it immediately went up to $20,000, then $30,000 then $40,000 and up until it sold for $98,000!

There was a bidding war between 4 people that had discovered that a museum needed one of these artist's works to fill their collection. So they all bid very high to gain access to the work of art, as they knew they could double the price later to the museum. This is very common in art dealing, people at the acquisitions department of museums, get donors to put together funds for acquisitions, and then they put a call out to dealers that they need to find a work of art by a certain artist.

The art dealers then advertise, network and anything then they do anything they can do to get a work of art by that artist. Then they make a deal with the museum, collector or other art dealer to make a sale.

L. Émile Adan

LOUIS EMILE ADAN 1839-1937
French, Genre, Landscape $15,000

Adler

JANKEL ADLER 1895-1949
Polish Painter, Portraits, Nudes $100,000

S. M. Adler

SAMUEL ADLER 1898-1979
American Modern $1,000

Edmund Adler

EDMUND ADLER 1871-1957
Austrian Painter $10,000

Andreenko

MIKHAIL ADREENKO 1894-1982
Russian Painter $5,000

Lucien Adrion

LUCIEN ADRION 1889-1953
French Painter $20,000

10

Tip: Don't Forget The Art Signature File
by G.B. David in Your Adventures!

Top Secret Technique 52
Regional Art treasure hunting

Regional areas have great markets and events that are very good buying opportunities for the Art Dealer that is willing to travel to these events. It can be an adventure and an amazing experience, as you get to see other parts of the country, and really get into the grass roots of the American experience. There is a great and well known flea market in the United States called Brimfield, in Massachusetts, and it is always talked about in the back rooms of art and antique dealers.

People that do Brimfield bring their best antiques and paintings, and sometimes will save up items for 6 months to take to the show. And most of the items are things that you have never seen before, sometimes things from the New England region, sometimes things from other parts of the country.

When you go to the event you see the whole town is involved with lodging and events, then on the day the market opens, people line up early in the morning waiting for the markets to open. There are several different markets on that day, so picking the right one is sometimes tricky. The anticipation is intense, as you can see the dealers in the open field setting up their items, and if you are with a partner working with you that day, you have to plan out who you will go to first, so you and your partner do not go to the same booth.

When the market opens everyone rushes in and tries to get the items they could see from the gate, hoping to get something good before their competitors get the item. I have found that if you rent a booth as a dealer this is the best way to get in the market before anyone else.

And you get to make deals privately before the gates open. Also if you have any paintings or works of art that you need to clear out, then you can put them in your booth, and have an assistant watch the booth, and then wander around and buy from the other dealers.

Also at night a lot of dealers get together for drinks, and food, socializing and it is great 2 or 3 day event, well worth the experience. These kinds of events go on all over the country; every community has antique flea market special sales, so it's good to keep up with these events. The Maine Antique Digest, and other great publications, usually list regional events, and it is a great source for finding where they are and when they will be held.

Sometimes being a part time weekend art dealer requires traveling to faraway places and meeting interesting people. It is the fun part of being an art dealer!

Top Secret Technique 53 Always take an Artist Price Guide with you on your Weekend Art excursions!

I like to use the Art Signature File as it has many artists, and artist signature samples, and has some pricing information so I can get an idea of the prices that the artists sells for at auction. This gives me a great advantage when I am out there looking for art.

It is available in ebook format through Kindle and has an easy search function that can search by just 3 letters, so if you cannot make out but 3 letters you can get close enough to see if it might be the way the artist signs.

The Art Signature File is a reference book of signatures of artists that have sold at auction, with information about the artist's and prices paid for the artist. It gives the, art lover, art researcher, collector, or art dealer the ability to look up artists names, and match signatures to the artist signatures on paintings, and other works of art.

Also you can get the Kindle app for your mobile phone for FREE, and then you can have The Art Signature File with you where ever you go, just in case you run into something!

Here are some excerpts from The Art Signature File price Guide by G.B. David it is a must have when you are traveling!

LOUIS EMILE ADAN 1839-1937
French, Genre, Landscape $15,000

JANKEL ADLER 1895-1949
Polish Painter, Portraits, Nudes $100,000

SAMUEL ADLER 1898-1979
American Modern $1,000

EDMUND ADLER 1871-1957
Austrian Painter $10,000

MIKHAIL ADREENKO 1894-1982
Russian Painter $5,000

LUCIEN ADRION 1889-1953
French Painter $20,000

10

Top Secret Technique 54 Economy gets worse then, more art gets discovered!

The worse the economy gets, the more opportunities become available for discovering art. The last thing a person wants during bad times is decorations, so attics, basements, and collections become available during bad times.

As a matter of fact some cultures over the years have looked down on art as a foolish investment, like China.

But it's amazing how now in current times their art is making records at auction, and they as people want to become artists, and collect art. The bad thing about down turns in the economy is that necessities take over with people that are not wealthy, and quite a few artworks wind up in the trash, because houses have to be sold, and storage spaces have to be vacated.

The world goes topsy turvy during these times and art takes a back seat to things that are needed. Only the rich and wealthy, are buying art during these times. And they are the ones that keep the art market going.

Even during the great depression many wealthy people were accumulating works of art, and most of those works are the most expensive works now in the museums.

So go out there fellow weekend art dealers, and save a work of art, look everywhere and try to keep the art from being tossed in the dumpster. Go to sales, yard sales, garage sales, and estate sales, and try to rescue the art, and in turn you will be helping someone out who has needs at this time also!

Top Secret Technique 55
The different levels of being an Art Dealer

There are many levels of being an art dealer, some art dealers will only deal in expensive works of art, where others deal in inexpensive works of art. The difference is that expensive art can make more money in a single sale, but it takes a lot more work to find it, identify it and to market it. And it is worth while of course. But art dealing in inexpensive artist's works can be a good business also. Every artist has cycles, and some artists like Jasper Johns get discovered immediately. But some artists take many years to be discovered, or appreciate as time goes by because their story, methods, or art becomes less available, or museums and collectors start buying up the artists works as soon as they become available.

Many times you will run into an art dealer or collector that asks all the other dealers do you have this artist, and then they try to corner the market on that artist by buying all the works they can get. Sometimes they will put advertisements in publications to buy this one artist and put high prices for the art. Then they buy all the art that is available which in turn pushes the price up on that artists works of art. This technique can also be used to buy styles, periods of art etc. Like an ad such as, "I would pay up to this amount for any Russian Avant

Garde work of art" so then dealers, antique dealers, art dealers, then look for those kinds of works of art, and try to acquire them, and then sell them to this person, or groups of people, who are buying this inventory.

This is how an inexpensive work of art by an artist can be placed into the expensive area of art. If no one can get a particular artists works, and museums and collectors have the desire for that work of art, then it is the simple law of supply and demand principle, the less supply, the more demand and the higher the price. So weekend art dealers should use these techniques, to deal, acquire, and sell and place art whenever they can.

Top Secret Technique 56
The best in art always seems to hold its value

Very important collectors realize that when they acquire a collection of art, they acquire only the best that the artist has created. This is one of the most successful tools of the weekend art collector and dealer. If you are lucky enough to be there when a great artist begins their career, you can amass a great art collection from the aspiring artist, and at the same time by funding the aspiring artist help their career. An example can be found in most all successful artist's stories of their life and relationships with art dealers and market makers.

Look at Mary Boone and her amazing career, many of her artists commanded over $1,000,000 prices. Mary Boone was an art dealer representing artists in the New York art market of the 1980s. Her list of artists included, Julian Schnabel, David Salle, Jean Michel Basquiat, Barbara Kruger, Eric Fischl, Ross Bleckner, and Brice Marden. Mary Boone was the first dealer to require waiting lists for collectors to buy works that had not yet been produced. Even though Picasso, who used to have dealers waiting in his waiting room at his studio would have gladly had dealers willing to be signed on to a waiting list also.

Leo Castelli was another Art Dealer artist market maker, with a vision. In 1957, he opened the Leo Castelli Gallery in a townhouse in New York City. He represented many soon to be high end artists such as: Wassily Kandinsky, Jackson Pollock, Willem de Kooning, Cy Twombly, Friedel Dzubas, and Norman Bluhm, Robert Rauschenberg, Frank Stella, Larry Poons, Lee Bontecou, James Rosenquist, Roy Lichtenstein, Andy Warhol, Robert Morris, Donald Judd, Dan Flavin, Cy Twombly, Ronald Davis, Bruce Nauman, Ed Ruscha, Salvatore Scarpitta, Richard Serra, Lawrence Weiner and Joseph Kosuth. He was fundamental in making markets for those artists all the way up to even today after his death.

And his wife Ileana Sonnabend started a gallery in Paris, and In the 1970s, she opened another contemporary art gallery in New York, the Sonnabend Gallery. And after she died at the age of 92, a portion of her art was sold for $600 million, and was considered the largest private sale of art in history.

And another important artist market maker was Peggy Guggenheim and most of the artists she associated with like Jackson Pollack. Some of the world's greatest art collections in museums have come from these exceptional art lovers who hung out with artists of greatness before they were great.

These art dealers and or market makers had one thing in common; they would help their careers along by buying, and acquiring their greatest works of art and supporting them along the way. Think about Jackson Pollack who has works that are selling at auction for tens of millions! He used to give drawings and paintings as payment for drinks and food in bars on Long Island, near East Hampton, New York.

Sometimes the best works of an artist are given to the closest friends of the artist. The works later acquired when the artist is discovered, can sometimes be lesser works in the sense that the artist may keep the best for himself, and sell only the works they feel they can do without.

Picasso was one of these artists but some of his best works were released as he went through his career. When creating a fine art collection it's important to acquire not only the great artist's works but also, the best of that artist's works.

Of course if you can acquire a Renoir work of art, or an artist of that importance, you will still be acquiring a valuable work, because of the rarity of the works available out there in the world!

Surrealism

The French author André Breton published "The Surrealist Manifesto" in 1924. The first Surrealist exhibition took place in 1925.

Some Surrealism artists

Agar, Eileen $12,500

Aragon, Louis $1000

Arp, Jean $450,000

Artaud, Antonin $70,000

Ball, Hugo

Bellmer, Hans $120,000

Boiffard, Jacques Andre

Brauner, Victor $350,000

Breton, Andre $240,000

Bunuel, Luis $5000

Burliuk, David $55,000

Carrington, Leonora $360,000

Cesariny, Mario

Chirico, Giorgio de $4,800,000

Cocteau, Jean $150,000

Cornell, Joseph $400,000

Top Secret Technique 57
Learn how to speak in Art Dealer language

When you are out there in the provinces, and you are looking for art, if the art is inexpensive then you need to use your art dealer knowledge, and experience to judge the buying of art. And then you should buy the art or not buy the art based on your expertise and judgment. Always ask yourself "can I sell this for more that I bought it for?" then after buying the art and never before buying the art, ask the seller questions like,

1.   Where did you get this from? (To maybe get some leads on the provenance or history of the art)

2.   Do you know who painted this?

3.   Do you have any others? Or any other pictures that I could look at?

Sometimes this last question gets many weekend art dealers into a whole new world, as the seller, might sometimes take you into your own private viewing of other works of art that the seller had put away to "check out" or to sell later on, or even to keep. Then you as an art dealer might have the chance to make a better deal on these better works of art. I have sometimes done this technique and I was led into a room that had several torn Hudson River paintings that were going to be thrown out at the end of the sale, and was able to acquire them for a few hundred dollars.

Always ask the questions, and only talk art dealer words if the work is an expensive item, as if you cannot afford to buy it, you could be part of earning a commission for selling the work of art for the seller, on consignment, in a gallery or at auction and everyone does well!

Top Secret Technique 58
How to manage, your art inventory wisely

It is a good idea to add a bar code sticker to your entire art inventory, so that you can have a way to identify your works of art. This helps if you have someone other than yourself when you are away, selling or showing your works of art.

The barcodes can be related to an excel worksheet where everything that you know about the work of art is listed there, like the artist if known, the size, the medium, the value you have determined, and the price that was paid, and a picture of the front and back and signature area, or marks, labels tags etc. This is also very good for insurance purposes, and can help in case of a fire or theft of the works of art.

Also when you put together or have shows, or you are showing your inventory to other dealers, galleries or auction houses it is an excellent way to manage your inventory.

Also this kind of inventory management adds to the ability of creating published catalogs of your collection that might be of interest when your collection grows, in the later years.

A good example is the Barnes collection, which is one of the most amazing collections of art in the world, and there have been many books describing that amazing collection of artworks.

Books were possible due to the amazing record keeping of the owner, and the protection he placed on his collection!

Some More Surrealism Artists

Crevel, Rene $1200

Dali, Salvador $4,126,680

Delvaux, Paul $4,500,000

Desnos, Robert $10,000

Dominguez, Oscar $300,000

Donati, Enrico $16,000

Duchamp, Marcel $1,762,500

Eluard, Paul $1200

Ernst, Max $2,429,500

Evans, Dulah Marie

Gepp, Gerhard

Giacometti, Alberto $103,900,000

Hayter, Stanley William $27,000

Hugnet, Georges $2500

Kamrowski, Gerome $1000

Klee, Paul $7,000,000

Leiris, Michel

Loy, Mina $1000

Top Secret Technique 59
Japanese Woodblock Bonanza

Japanese wood block prints were very available right after World War II and soldiers picked them up for 25 cents and brought them back to the USA where they went on walls, attics, basements etc.

Today these wood block prints are very valuable, and some have gone for over $100,000 at auction.

There are different qualities and aspects related to the collecting and dealing of antique wood block prints, and there are contemporary artists in china and in Japan still creating works of art in this medium that are now getting good prices at auction.

One of the best places to make a deal on Japanese woodblocks is Ronin Gallery.

I got this from their website... it says:

"Whether you are selling select works, an entire collection, or simply want to learn more about your art, we are always happy to help. Please send high quality photos, any detailed information you may have, and your contact information (phone number and email) to ronin@roningallery.com.

Value is determined by the artist, condition, state or edition of the work, overall design, rarity and the art market at any given time.

This is a link to their site:

http://www.roningallery.com/

You can learn a lot about woodblock prints by just browsing their website.

You can contact the Gallery located at:

425 Madison Avenue
3rd Floor, SE corner of 49th St.
New York, NY 10017

212.688.0188

They are extremely nice people and will be glad to assist you in your woodblock print selling, buying, and education.

Top Secret Technique 60
The different mediums Art is created in Materials and Techniques of artworks

Here are some reasons that you might need a conservator to help you in analyzing works of art on paper and paints inks etc. Here is a little information about those mediums.

Before the advent of the pencil, artists making finely detailed drawings had to rely on a metal stylus dragged across a coated paper.

The use of a pencil was changed by the politics of wars in the 1800's which blocked the trade with England in graphite, and this lead to the use artificial graphite in the late 1700's.

It is easy to identify both these forms of graphite using special imaging.

A drawing with artificial graphite cannot be dated earlier than the late 1700's.

Many modern works of art are difficult to analyze and date as they use the modern pencils.

The many kinds of artworks that art dealers sometimes deal in are:

Painting

Sculpture

Installation art

Photography

Conceptual art

Drawing

Printmaking

Performance art

Video art

Ceramics

4-D art

Land art

New Media art

Collage

Assemblage

In ancient drawings done with metal points on coated paper, the metal in the media can oxidize, causing a change in color. For example, a silver point drawing may become tarnished to black or copper point to green. This may cause a piece to be misidentified.

Silver point can be reconverted to its original appearance by exposure to hydrogen peroxide. Ink, has often been used as writing, painting and printing medium, although it is usually applied in thin washes rather than thick impasto. Inks low in carbon, like bistre, become invisible when examined under infrared illumination.

Paintings can have many types of colors such as tempera, gouache, watercolor, oil and acrylic. For example, gouache differs from water color in that it is an opaque medium, whereas water color is transparent. In watercolor the white or highlights come from the background paper, but in gouache the white is applied as a pigment.

Gouache is sometimes used for impasto effects and this extra thickness causes a major problem with gouache media. It can crack, scratch, rub, and become abrasive. Tempera is a generic term for any aqueous media that "tempers" or binds pigment with egg, glue, gum, or starch.

Egg tempera, used primarily between the 10th and 15th centuries (replaced encaustic until artists used oil paint) regained popularity in the 19th century. Egg tempera consists primarily of egg yolk, which is a natural emulsion containing a drying oil that can take up to a year to dry. The use of temper was replaced by gouache between the 16th and 18th centuries for illuminated manuscripts.

Gouache is often confused with watercolor. Watercolor differs from gouache in composition (having no white filler for body or highlights), Watercolor became established in the 18th century, used to illuminate books and manuscripts where the fugitive nature of such a lean medium would be protected. Printing There are several major categories of prints: relief, intaglio, planographic, stencil, and photomechanical.

Relief prints are made by carving away areas of a printing block, usually wooden, to leave raised areas that carry the ink. When the block is placed in contact with a piece of paper and pressed or rubbed, the ink is pressed into the paper, sometimes actually indenting or impressing the paper slightly.

This is especially apparent in Japanese woodblock prints or in letterpress prints found in early broadsides and newspapers. The major problem with relief prints is that this distinct impression around the inked areas, evidence of relief techniques, could be flatten or lost if improperly cared for or treated.

Intaglio prints are made by incising a plate, usually metal, by any of several processes. The incisions are filled with ink, and the plate is wiped so that the surface is clean.

The plate is then inverted onto a damp piece of paper and run through a press to force ink to sit on top of the paper. Planographic prints, usually monotypes or lithographs, are created by placing a flat substrate, such as litho stone or piece of glass, with an inked design coating the surface, against a piece of paper and exerting pressure.

This technique is often used to imitate other media such as drawings the stencil process involves allowing ink or paint to come in contact with only the design areas of the paper by essentially blocking the negative areas of the paper in a variety of ways.

The ink is brushed or squeezed onto the paper around the negative space or through a blocked screen. Edges of image color often have little pinholes from burst air bubbles in squeezed paint. Photomechanical prints are distinguished from "fine arts" prints in several ways. Fine arts prints are hand-pulled in limited editions since the quality of printed image eventually changes as printing plates wear down.

Art Deco

Art Deco refers generally to the decorative arts of the 1920s and 1930s a famous artist Erté, who is known as the 'father of Art Deco.'

Some Art Deco artists

Alen, William van

Artigas, Joan-Gardy $1000

Cappiello, Leonetto $9500

Cassandre, Adolphe Mouron $21,000

Dreyfuss, Henry

Drtikol, Frantisek $59,000

Erté Tirtoff, Romain de $35,000

Follot, Paul $1000

Lalique, Rene $55,000

Lempicka, Tamara de $8,500,000

Ragan, Leslie $11,000

Top Secret Technique 61
How to view an Artwork for maximum discovery

Always look at all aspects of a work of art; if it is a painting then you should look at the front first, then the back, then the edges or sides. Look on the front for the age of the paint, the style of the art, see if there is a signature or mark that the artist might have used to sign the work of art.

Then look at the back of the work of art and see if the painting on the front matches the age of the back, things to look for would be the color of the stretcher if it is a painting on canvas, or the color and condition of the art board surface if it was a painting on board.

Also on the back see if there are any signatures on the stretcher, or canvas, also look to see if there is any restoration to damage that can be seen from the back.

Another thing to try to determine is was this painting relined, in restoration that is a very costly part of restoration, and most of the time that means that the work of art warrants that cost, or that the work of art is valuable.

Now we need to look at the edges, are all the nails that hold the canvas to the stretcher in the same original holes, or are they next to old holes, and then look at the nails are they new, or are they old, and then look at the shape of the nail heads are they perfectly round or different shapes which would mean they are very old.

A lot can be determined when looking at a painting or work of art that will help in the research of the painting later on. You should always make notes and sketches in your art dealer's research book, that has an image attached so that you can easily get to the information, when you are researching, at your computer on the net, or in a research library, in a museum or private art reference library.

Top Secret Technique 62
Art Dealing is something like a trumpet. If you don't put anything in, you won't get anything out

Being an art dealer part time or full time, you need to buy art, store art, and sell art that is the nature of the business. So if you do not buy art, you cannot sell art generally speaking.

But there are exceptions to the rules, as some art dealers will take artist works on consignment, for the shows they make, or in their online catalogues for sale. So you can actually be an art dealer that does not control the storage, or handling of the art, if you have an online art dealer brokerage.

It's easy to make a deal with a modern or contemporary artist to sell their works when an artist is just starting out. Some of the greatest art dealers of all time did just this, and they made their careers off being the first ones to make these kinds of deals.

But the art dealer should have some inventory, to sell, and the art dealer should be able to physically show art to a potential buyer at any time. Also its just good business sense to fulfill the other needs of the art dealer and that is the buyers; you need to cultivate your buyer's. Everyone that you meet should know that you are an art dealer, and you should always have a card to give potential buyers. As an art dealer you should always be up on the current trends and art markets, as some buyers buy because they use art as an investment. Also if you are an art market maker, you should be able to explain why you feel a certain artist works will be more valuable in the future, so that you can tell buyers, why you think they should have these works in their collections.

Networking is a big part of becoming a successful art dealer, and you should let everyone know this is something you take seriously. But also be aware that art buyers sometimes buy because they like the subject, style, impact and size of the art work, along with the story behind the artist who creates the art work. These are very compelling sales strategies, and should be planned out thoroughly for presentations when the subject comes up. When someone says, "So you are an art dealer? That sounds exciting, who is the hot artist now?" you should be able to tell them something that is very compelling and interesting. Plan out your artists that you are selling be an expert in their lives, and know the market like a professional, and you will not go wrong.

Top Secret Technique 63
When buying Art don't worry about failure. Worry about the chances you miss when you don't even try

Be confident in yourself as an art buyer, and remember confidence comes from experience. So always test your art in sales, and reactions from buyers. You should not worry about art buying mistakes, as you go along you will be stuck with mistakes, in inventory of art that you can not sell.

But sooner or later, you will be able to seasonally clear out your inventory of mistakes, and that inventory will diminish as you trade art over time.

Its like anything else one does in the world, the more you do it the more you get better at it. If your budget is limited in the beginning then maybe the best way to start is to represent newer artist on consignment.

Just sign an exclusive deal with an aspiring artist and market their works for a period of time on a consignment method. You take certain artworks and then try to sell them, then return them if they do not sell.

You get a certain percentage for the sales, and you learn a lot about being a true art dealer and art market maker. Not to say that you can't be buying art, storing, showing and selling it at higher profits later on. That can always come along the way, remember if you saw a work of art at a sale and it was only $20 and you sold it for $1500 that's not a big investment and that would be a great art deal! It happens every day, and it can happen to you!

Top Secret Technique 64
Every great achievement was once impossible until an individual set a goal to make it a reality

Do not give up on your art dealer achievements, you can do it, it can be very rewarding, and exciting in meeting new people, and going to exciting places. Every achievement in this profession whether it be full time or part time, is a real achievement. And many art dealers have made and changed history, as every art work that is discovered ads to the wealth of information about the art and the artist who created that artwork.

Sometimes even changing the way the art community looks at the methods, and reasons that artist's create. There are many instances where art research in museums, gives us new information as to the artists life, and methods that we never knew.

There have actually been cases that were resolved by methods in art research, and ways of thinking discovered as in the Da Vinci code, and other forms of expression hidden in the art that is created!

Art Nouveau

The Art nouveau movement 1880's – 1905 originated in London and was also called sezessionstil in Austria, jugendstil in Germany, and modernismo in Spain.

Some Art Nouveau Artists

Beardsley, Aubrey $49,000

Behrens, Peter $2000

Berlage, Hendrik

de Feure, Georges $165,000

Eckmann, Otto

Endell, August

Gaudi, Antoni $15,000

Giacometti, Diego $90,000

Guimard, Hector

Horta, Victor

Klimt, Gustav $135,000,000

Klinger, Max $37,000

Lalique, Rene $55,000

Mackintosh, Charles $360,000

Mucha, Alphonse $100,000

Obrist, Hermann $1000

Riemerschmid, Richard $2500

Top Secret Technique 65 Schedule independent art research time and free time

When you are researching art works that you cannot figure out, remember that around 60% are works of art that need to be researched before they can be sold.

But that is not always accurate, as sometimes, an art dealer can just take a work of art into a gallery, art auction house, or another dealer, and they know right away who the artist is, or they will take it in for research and let you know.

But on those works of art that you have to research yourself, remember you are doing this on a part time basis, and if it is not fun then why do it?

So allocate a certain amount of time for art research, and balance that against your free time. Also make your art research not so confined to your home art dealer office, but make excursions into the libraries, research departments of museum libraries, and other places, so you can have a fun adventure.

And when you finally figure out who the artist is, or when the work of art was created etc. try not to scream out loud, as the art reference libraries are serious places. But believe me I know the feeling when the final discovery moment comes and it is a very nice moment.

Just have fun, and know that every art research project will lead to a new understanding of art, for you and will add to your knowledge of art, and will also add to your bank account, and this is what fun is!

Top Secret Technique 66
Build a supportive community and nurture it, every day

Talk with your family and friends about your adventures in your art dealer travels, as this makes for interesting and exciting discussions. Also you should have parties and get togethers, and invite people that are your peers in art dealing. Your children will find it interesting to see how people create art and the history behind most of the art movements.

The one thing that separates us from the animals is that we as humans have the need to be creative. And it's always exciting to see the creative things that humans make, and sometimes live their lives around creating.

An artist is a very peculiar human, most of them, that are famous or about to be famous have dedicated their life to their art. These unusual humans believe in what they do so much that they often go through long periods of time creating the same style of art. Most of these people do not do it for money; actually the majority of artists do it for self fulfillment of their ideas.

Only very few were able to see their works of art sell for outrageous amounts in their lifetime. The real artist sees a vision and has to create it immediately, so that the vision can be a reality. All of these things about artist should be an inspiration to your family and friends, and colleagues, to aspire to be better people. We can learn a lot from these creationists, the artist, and their processes!

Top Secret Technique 67
Manage your thoughts, and the way you look at an artwork

Be careful when looking at art, as sometimes things that are apparent are not real. There are many forgers, and art fakers today, and you need to be very careful in works that you find out there. You should manage your thoughts and be very analytical and realistic about the works of art that you are buying.

First always know that if someone is willing to sell you an original Monet painting where the signature is very legible, and they only want $20 to $100 and the painting look very old and legitimate, you might have to buy it, even though you may later on have to hang it on your wall, or sell it as a fake. If the Monet is being sold for thousands of dollars, then most likely it's not real or stolen. But that is not always the case, so you should buy wisely, and manage your thoughts, do not get emotional, do not let ego get in the way of your decisions.

Like a samurai think wisely, make a decision, and execute the decision, not having any regrets after you make your decision even if it goes bad. Another aspect of how to deal with the thousands of dollars Monet is that you can propose signing a consignment agreement, and let the seller know that you would like to verify the authenticity of the work of art, and then you would like to split the profits over what they were asking that you can surely get for them.

This path generally will bring out whether the seller is a faker, a forger, a person that has already checked the work out and knows that it is a fake, or a person that just has no knowledge of anything about the art work.

So if they are real, then they would not object to letting you research the work of art, and possibly getting more than what they were asking. It's all about your attitude, and your professionalism, to be able to make a deal like this. But you can do it, and it only costs you visit to an expert, which in the case of Monet most towns have someone in a museum, or gallery that can do this.

Top Secret Technique 68
Life is a daring adventure, in art dealing or nothing

Art dealing is a great adventure, and you have to dare to make it work for you. That is why it is important to have a portion of your part time art dealing involving new artists in your community. Go out meet them at shows, have dinner with them, socialize and sign up deals to market their art. Dedicate at least 20% of your art dealing career to this endeavor. In the end you will make deals, and you will build relationships with some of the most exciting people on this planet. Remember if you do not have art to sell then you are not an art dealer, and this 20% of your time will get you a large amount of art to sell. Even if you get only 10 artists that you represent on a part time basis. The amounts of art that you can represent and sell will be quite a bit. And if you can put on occasional group shows that can help you make more revenue, and can be a nice time outing for your family, friends and you're colleagues who should all be on your invitation list, imagine your children will be delighted to get an invitation to a group exhibition from you in the mail.

Also to help finance the group exhibitions you can set up a way where the costs of the show can be divided between the artists and you. And you can add a blog for the show, and link into facebook and twitter before and from the show.

Also it's a good idea to video tape the event, and video tape the artists discussing their works of art at a pre show and during the show event. And this video can be used later on for collateral promotions, DVD's, you tube, and other promotional concepts for generating more funds for producing more group shows.

Of course there should be refreshments, food, music, and brochures, business cards at the events. Some of the best art was shown in these kinds of venues in 1920's 1940's with artists that had never been seen before, and this leads to these artists to be collected by many an art lover.

Remember "Life is a daring adventure, in art dealing or nothing" so make it a very daring adventure, be an alpha leader and guide your flock of artists to their being known!

Top Secret Technique 69
Put your money where it will reap the most rewards

Always put your money on smart and profitable investments in art acquisitions. Try to make sure you are not stuck with art that used up your capital that you can not sell.

You should liquidate these items as soon as possible. Of course the exception to the rule is fine art that has a value, which takes time to sell. This art should be stored and kept until it will sell.

But in the beginning artworks that are acquired by beginning art dealers, include many mistakes, and I have seen many art dealers, that have a routine to analyze their mistakes in their storage area, and sell them at a flea market at bargain basement prices, or at a garage sale, or yard sell, to liquefy their frozen assets like every 3 months.

Also I have known many part time art dealers that will take all their art acquisition mistakes that have been researched and bunch them together in one ebay or online auction sale, or sell them to another art dealer that might be interested for some reason.

You should always be open to these tactics, and make it a regular habit, it is a good way to clean your inventory of personal art buys, and get cash that can be used for more smart buying so that your churn rate of art coming in and going out can be maintained in a healthy way. But always check your acquisitions out thoroughly, as you do not want to make a $10,000 mistake!

Blaue Reiter

The Blaue Reiter movement was from 1911 to 1914 in Germany.

Some Artists of the Blaue Reiter

Beckmann, Max $3,200,000

Bloch, Albert $134,000

Campendonck, Heinrich Campendonk $325,000

Jawlensky, Alexej von $8,296,000

Kandinsky, Wassily $40,000,000

Klee, Paul $7,000,000

Macke, August $3,810,040

Marc, Franz $5,061,500

Werefkin, Marianne von $24,000

Top Secret Technique 70
Is it the right time to sell that work of art?

One time there was this weekend art dealer who had been very lucky in finding a valuable painting. The Artist had listings of $50,000, and he decided to sell it, because he purchased it for very little. The art market at that time was, great, but the galleries were not purchasing, because the economy was tightening.

The dealer went from gallery to gallery, and he tried all the usual Top Secret Techniques to sell his work of art, but all he could get was a $30,000 offer. Being a smart dealer and knowing that the work was worth much more he held on to the art for a couple of more months.

And the $30,000 offer actually dwindled to $20,000 from some interests he was contacting. Now this dealer felt maybe he should take the $20,000, but just as he was going to accept the offer, he found out that the artist that painted the work of art, had a new international sales record set of $200,000!

So because the dealer was vigilant and determined, he held off selling, and was able to get much more for the exceptional work of art. Things in the Art world are changing constantly, and this is how the art dealer can purchase a work of art for a song and sell it for a fortune! But sometimes we can be distracted by the economical times and get caught not selling at the right time, or selling at the right time.

The decision is made with the information we have at the time we decide to sell. We have to be happy at the outcome, and not LOOK BACK! Many a dealer has become a collector, because they have sold something in the past that today is worth a fortune! To be profitable, you have to move 60% of your acquisitions, and if you want to collect hold onto 40% as a rule!

Top Secret Technique 71
Control the cash that you use, to spend on art!

Always make sure you have some cash on the weekends set aside for the occasional art deal as you never know when you are going to run into something that is an opportunity in acquiring art works.

Never get into the sad event where you have discovered a work of art for $300 that can be sold for $3000 and not have a way to be able to lock the deal down. So always have at least $300 set aside somewhere and actually should be with you when you are out on your art seeking adventures.

But also remember to manage your inventory wisely, and make sure you not only buy but that you set aside time each week or every other week for selling your art a business needs inflow of funds as well as outflow of funds, and the business of art dealing needs to be managed wisely.

As an art dealer should have just the right amount of liquidity. And also you should set up a backup plan with other art dealer colleagues, that if you are short funds to make deals that they will work with you on a split of the profits in a deal that they help you fund.

This backup plan can also work when in your travels you come upon a loaded dumpster with art, or a sale with so much art that you cannot get it, and you might need 2 other dealers with their entourage to help. But always state what the deal is and what percentage you want for your finder's fee.

Top Secret Technique 72 Dedicate at least two hours a week to, marketing your art

You should do marketing of art at least 2 hours every week, whether it be adding blog pages to your art dealer blog, or adding marketing information to your artists art inventory on your online gallery web page. Or even marketing in Val Pak in a mailing, or just doing a mailing yourself to potential buyers directly about your art brokerage business inventory.

It could even be an online newsletter, or mailed newsletter. Remember if it is mailed to the right targeted buyers, you could make some nice deals. Also being a wholesaler middle art dealer is a possibility, as stores, and galleries are looking for new items to sell all the time, and if you have a contract with a particular artist that is desired in the stores, you can make some nice deals.

Always respond back to inquiries in a timely fashion as an inquiry is half the sale and people would not be inquiring if they were not thinking of things. Sometimes you can leads into collections of art for sale from you advertising efforts!

Bauhaus

The Bauhaus movement was founded in Germany 1919 and continued till 1933.

Some Artists of the Bauhaus

Albers, Josef $1,136,000

Albers, Anni $8500

Bayer, Herbert $60,000

Behrens, Peter $2000

Bill, Max $57,000

Breuer, Marcel $2500

Citroen, Paul $25,000

Feininger, Andreas $41,000

Feininger, Lyonel $7,688,888

Feininger, T Lux $4500

Gropius, Walter $1300

Henri, Florence $4500

Itten, Johannes $25,000

Kandinsky, Wassily $40,000,000

Klee, Paul $7,000,000

Marcks, Gerhard $40,000

Mies van der Rohe, Ludwig

Moholy, Lucia

Moholy-Nagy, Laszlo $5000

Top Secret Technique 73 Equalize your sales of art and profit goals

Set goals for your art sales that will match the profit goals that you set. You should setup systems that enable you, to be able to sell as much art as you can. These systems setup should include:

1.   Blogging in many blogs about the artists that you are currently representing, and you collection of art that you are selling from.

2.   Auctions online and offline that you are currently consigning to. There are over 50 online auctions where you can sell your art, and many offline auctions that exist.

3.   Your Website, it does not take much of an expense these days to have a website created or you can create it yourself. You should have all the art that you are selling with daily updates on artists that you represent.

4.   Stationery is important, some people feel that printed advertising is old fashioned, but it is not. Business cards, flyers, mailing pieces and anything that you can use to spread the word about your art should be used. Remember the people that

generally buy art are unapproachable, they spend their time not being able to be solicited, and that is why mailings sometimes can get to these people.

5. Magazine, newspaper, and print media advertising, you should find regional and trade publications to advertise your art brokerage in. always include your website. But remember to be a smart advertiser; do not spend too much on these kinds of marketing.

6. Facebook, Twitter, and many other social networking online venues can work if you do it right. I know an artist who has been very successful at marketing his own art through these venues. And has quite a following of people that follow his career and occasionally buy from him. I also know of another artist that paints nice pictures that has sold online for years, and actually makes a living doing just that.

7. Viral Marketing is the most cost effective form of advertising that is in existence today. With viral marketing the art dealer can get major press coverage and focus into their brokerage website. All the art dealer has to do is represent an up and coming artist that might be a little flamboyant, or different in their art or the way they live or think. Then make an outrageous video, and place it on You Tube and if it is interesting or entertaining then

that artist could be an overnight sensation. And then their art will be flying out the door with sales figures climbing. Remember to get a contract for your representation of artists, and make sure that the art from your viral video, and website, that you make for them, or they have covers art sales, for your commissions.

8.   Art liquidation of multiple works of art for one price, in flea markets, garage sales, yard sales, galleries, online auctions, and stores.

All of these techniques combined listed above should be used systematically for you to reach your profit goals, and sales amounts. By using the right combination of the above you can reach those goals easily!

Rayonism

The Rayonism or Cubo-Futurism movement during the 1910's was the beginning of abstract art in Russia and was founded by Mikhail F. Larionov and his wife Natalia Goncharova.

Artists of the Rayonism movement

Goncharova, Natalia $10,870,500
Larionov, Mikhail $3,200,000

Top Secret Technique 74
Every dollar in art expense should be directly tied to greater cash income Formula

One technique that most art dealers use is that they do not buy art just to put it on their wall. Most of the time at the moment of every dollar spent on art, or later on, they establish a sales target for that work of art. Either in their head or written down in their art research notebook, they establish the price they think they can get for the art.

One technique that is often used is to mark 4 prices down:

1. The price the work of art was purchased for originally by the art dealer.
2. The price that the art dealer feels that they can get in a sale of the art.
3. The price that the art dealer would accept for the art, which would be less than the number 2 price.
4. The price that will be the starting price for the art work, at sale, auction, or direct marketing.

So an example of the way this would work would be that say you purchased a work of art at a garage sale for $40, and you think you can get $200 for that work of art. Then you would say but if I was to sell it for $100 that is not too bad, say a 60% profit. And you're starting price to ask would be $300, as you never know you might actually get a buy it now, from someone who just must have it at that time. Or directly from a buyer, who does not ask for a lower price, and just buys the work of art.

Given that these are the figures that you want to work with and you set as your buy and sell targets:

1.   1=$40
2.   2=$200
3.   3=$100
4.   4=$300

Then your profit for your art brokerage will always be represented in percentages of profits as related to dollar sales. And the formula would be:

1.   1 = % of 3 = A
2.   1 = % of 2 = B
3.   1 = % of 4 = C

A. 60% at the low, for mistakes, or need to sell, or even [represented artists which could actually change this formula as you might only be able to get 20% to 35% of new artists works that you represent, but you would not have an expense except for the costs of shows promotions etc which actually could be offset by having artists pay for their share of the group shows].

B. 500% that you will anticipate if you are a good buyer and you know what you can sell your owned artworks for.

C. over 700% if you get a great buyer or you greatly misjudged the value.

So you have setup your art dealer business with the criteria for the art profits, and you should always adhere to these price points. Of course as you learn more and more these price points will be achieved easier. And you have to set the formula prices for what you feel you can get. By sticking to your cash income formula for your business, and always keeping up with current market values from art auctions, and gallery shows, you will reap the joys and rewards of being an art dealer much easier and faster!

Cubism

The Cubism movement which included artist's who were active between 1907 and 1914, was created mainly by the painters Pablo Picasso and Georges Braque in Paris.

Some Artists of the Cubism movement

Adler, Jankel $104,000

Archipenko, Alexander $2,667,408

Braque, Georges $8,640,000

Delaunay, Robert $5,170,000

Duchamp-Villon, Raymond $1,762,500

Fauconnier, Henri le $45,000

Gris, Juan $8,479,500

Laurens, Henri $1,472,000

Leger, Fernand $22,407,500

Lipchitz, Jacques $1,300,000

Marcoussis, Louis $385,000

Metzinger, Jean $700.000

Picasso, Pablo $106,500,000

Rozanova, Olga $300,000

Udaltsova, Nadezhda Andreevna $20,000

Top Secret Technique 75
The ultimate profitable weekend art dealer micro business

Imagine you can set up a business on a part time basis that can be run from your home, with no additional expenses, or very little additional expenses. Plus it only takes up maybe an hour or 2 on Saturday and Sunday or both. And you can have fun going from yard sale, to garage sale, to flea markets looking for artworks. Or meeting with potential artists that you want to represent in their studios, or at coffee shops, or invite them over for breakfast, lunch or dinner. Also getting your 10 artists that you want to represent, and setting up group shows, and going to group shows, in the afternoon or evening, meeting people and having a lot of esthetic fun.

There is a certain Zen from being able to help aspiring artists, and placing works of fine art, from past artists, which is very, self rewarding. You can do this, anyone can do this, the overhead is low, and the learning is high and an everyday learning experience, and the experience that is gained from this business is good for a lifetime for you and your family, and friends!

Les Nabis, "The Nabis"

Nabis, which means prophet, and was created in the 1890s, by Paul Serusier and Maurice Denis.

Some Artists of Les Nabis

Bonnard, Pierre $8,528,000

Denis, Maurice $385,000

Maillol, Aristide $2,800,000

Serusier, Paul $400,000

Vallotton, Felix $465,000

Vuillard, Eduard $7,481,481

Top Secret Technique 76
Do not even think about leaving FUN out of the formula for success in your weekend art business

When you have your first sale up on line for your art, or you produce your first group artist's show, or you sell your first work of art at Sothebys or Christies, you will see the fun in being an art dealer. But even when you are up early on a Saturday to be at the local flea market with your coffee in hand and running from booth to booth, with an art adventure about to begin, there is an element of satisfaction, and fun even if that day you come up short in your art hunt.

And sometimes even going out later in the day can be rewarding fun, as not all the art that is for sale out there gets bought in the mornings and there are still works of art left later on in the day. You will notice that the sellers are more reasonable then and will drop the prices much more readily later in the day.

As the day goes by less people come by to view the items for sale at garage sales, yard sales, and flea markets.

The thought is that if the art was any good then it would not still be here. But depending on what you use in your system for selling art, you may have a way to market these works of art, and you might be able to get a bargain.

Also remember that you can have a catalog of your personal art that you own for sale, placed at your group shows for new artists that you represent. So that potential buyers might contact you after the show, to look at your art collection for possible purchases, so even at the end of the day on Saturday or Sunday, you can have fun acquiring art works and maybe even get some bargains!

Top Secret Technique 77 Master your art research and reference tools, including the way you think

Art reference tools are very important; to an art dealer any price guides, or images of art works, or signature books, should be acquired first of all. One reason to get these tools in your library, is that traveling to museum libraries, or university libraries takes time, and its good to be able to work from the comfort of your home. If your budget is limited in the beginning, then just start out with something like The Art Signature File on ebook Kindle, iPad its only $9.95 and it has many signature, prices, and artist to look for, but really gives you a good start in research, then later on you can get used, Sotheby's and Christies art catalogs that are inexpensive.

And then you should try to get Davenport's price guide, and Mayer's price guides, of works of art at auction which are hundreds of dollars but worth it. And there are on line art reference materials that have subscription services, when you get more profits in your art dealer business. Remember the way you think is important in your art dealing business; you have to be sure to be confident that you can sell the art that you acquire.

And you have to be always setting up networks and channels for selling your art works. The New artist that you have contracted to sell for, need to know that mentally you are with them in promoting their art and selling their art for them.

They need to feel like that you will be a part of their career for many years. So mentally make them understand that you like their works of art, and work out constructive discussion sessions over dinner or coffee about what they need to do to make your ability to sell even better.

The mental relationship between you and your art, and artists that you represent is an important part of becoming an art dealer. Remember leave the ego out, and also know that being an artist is an ego related thing, and do not make the mistake of getting into that mental ego area of debate. It is bad for your art dealing business, and your sales of artists works!

Top Secret Technique 78
Be passionate with your Art Research and Dealing

People will know if you are really passionate about the artists you represent and their artworks, and the whole art field in general. So always be true to your feelings and likes and dislikes about the art and artists you represent.

Make that passion come across in the sales of art works, show your buyers that you truly like the art that you sell and represent, never doubt your decisions in your representations. Also in the same are of thought, be passionate in your research to gain the knowledge of works of art.

Always ask yourself what is it about how the art was created, and the subject, that the artist was trying to get across. Try to get into the artists head to be able to understand who the artist was in your research.

And always have a passion to get the work of art placed, and hopefully in a collection where the art can be seen over and over for years to come, by the public.

This is the only protection for artworks created by humans, so that they will be passed down to the next generations, for people to see and learn what people were creating, and inspire them to create also, and wonder about us as a civilization. This is the passion of being an art dealer, plus you have to love art!

Vorticism

The British movement Vorticism was active between 1912 and 1915, and was a combination of Futurism and Cubism.

Some Artists of Vorticism

Atkinson, Lawrence $25,000

Bomberg, David $1,916,981

Dismorr, Jessica $6000

Epstein, Jacob $60,000

Gaudier Brzeska, Henri $27,000

Lewis, Wyndham $30,000

Roberts, William

Wadsworth, Edward $120,000

Top Secret Technique 79
Focus on your strengths

In your art dealer business always focus on your strengths and eliminate your weaknesses when handling the things you can do for your business. Sometimes you have to rely on experts, like appraisers, curators, collectors, gallery owners, restoration people, and other professionals. Understand that if you do not have the skills for restoration, research, buying and selling, then you need to get someone else to do these things, until you can learn how to do some or all of these things.

Focus on your strengths, that will make your art dealer business successful and delegate to other people either on a permanent basis or temporary basis, and you will have a successful art dealer business!

Post Impressionism

The Post Impressionism movement was between 1880 and 1890's.

Some Artists of Post Impressionism

Bonnard, Pierre $8,528,000

Cezanne, Paul $60,500,000

Dufy, Jean $100,000

Evans, Dulah Marie

Gauguin, Paul $40,330,000

Gogh, Vincent van $82,500,000

Jones, Judy

Krehbiel, Albert $1300

Matar, Joseph

Monet, Claude $80,000,000

Renoir, Pierre-Auguste $78,100,000

Rohlfs, Christian $100,000

Serusier, Paul $400,000

Signac, Paul $2,692,000

Spencer, Stanley $2,307,690

Vuillard, Eduard $7,481,481

Top Secret Technique 80
Never consider the possibility of failure in, your art research

In researching art failure should never be an option when you are trying to determine the artists that have created a particular work of art. Only works that have no marks or signatures are difficult research projects, but even these works can be identified.

As a matter of fact there are many works of art that have been identified that were old master works of a particular school of art that go for tens of thousands of dollars, without a signature!

These works of art are classified as "from the school of" and are very desirable, as they may some day be proven to be one of the masters of fine art, by further research methods.

So always understand that identification can be done on anything. It just takes a few tests, like age, style and medium. And you can identify any work of art and make it sellable.

If you are stumped at the identification of an artwork another technique that is widely used is to show it to your art dealer and antique dealer peers and colleagues.

They will be happy to show off their talents and knowledge, and who knows they might even in the end want to make a deal with you on the sale of the work of art you are researching! Remember failure is not even an option!

Cobra

The Cobra art movement between 1948 and 1951 began in Denmark. Named comes from, COpenhagen, BRussels and Amsterdam. Cobra was an art movement that emulated childhood creativity and children's art styles for the purpose of expressing freedom from previous art periods.

Some Artists of Cobra

Alechinsky, Pierre $2,000,000
Alfelt, Else
Appel, Karel $100,000
Balle, Mogens $8500
Bille, Ejler
Brands, Eugene
Bury, Pol $27,000
Corneille Guillaume $100,000
Cox, Jan $25,000
d'Haese, Reinhoud
Diederen, Jef
Dotremont, Christian
Gaag, Lotti van der $2500

Top Secret Technique 81
Look for ways to network in the art world

Networking in the art world is a joy and a necessity. You must set these networks up as a priority for starting your new art dealer brokerage business.

1. Go to any art dealer groups and join, or read the posts, using a search in Google like:

   A. http://www.linkedin.com/groups/Art-Dealers-Network-1872358

   B. http://www.linkedin.com/groups/Private-Art-Dealers-Network-2700338

   C. http://www.artdealers.org/members.last.html

   D. http://art.meetup.com/

   E. http://www.washingtonartdealers.org/html_pages/newsandevents.html

2. Check in your local community for meetup groups, and art discussion groups.

3.   Visit many antique dealers if not all of them in your area, start by asking them about their paintings and sculptures they are selling. Find out all about them, so you can learn the prices and what they are selling.

4.   Ask the antique dealers if you can get a commission if you sell some of their works of art for them.

5.   Start going to art galleries and talk with the directors, telling them that you are an independent art dealer, and that you have client that might be interested in purchasing some of their works. And you need to know what your commission for sales would be.

6.   Go to new artist shows and try to meet the artists that do works of art that you really like, even though some might have exclusive contracts with other dealers you might find some that will give you an opportunity to sell their art for them. Invite them over for dinner, and discuss the possibility of group shows and marketing events you have planned.

7.   Put an ad in the local university, for art major students, or people interested in art for possible research in art works that you have or discussions of art movements, and styles etc.

Some More Cobra Artists

Heerup, Henry $10,000

Heusch, Luc de

Jacobsen, Robert $60,000

Jorn, Asger $2,099,500

Kouwenaar, Gerrit

Lindstrom, Bengt $22,000

Lucebert $50,000

Ortvad, Erik $20,000

Pedersen, Carl-Henning

Rooskens, Anton $45,000

Tajiri, Shinkichi

Thommesen, Erik

Vandercam, Serge $2800

Top Secret Technique 82
Use the Internet often for art information

The internet is a great place with huge amounts of information, so use it a lot in your art research, and for setting up art sales.

Some sites even have mobile apps that you can use with your mobile phone, when you are out in the provinces and countryside, on your art hunting adventures. Let's say that you see a name on the back of a stretcher of a painting on canvas.

You can immediately go to Google with your mobile phone and search for that name.

It might be the artist, or it could be the framer, or another famous collector, but this information can be the difference in the amount that you pay for that work of art.

Also if you can identify names on frames and stretchers, always remember to put them in your art dealer research notebook for further reference to down the road.

Also the Internet is a great place to get colleagues, and experts to help you in identification of artworks, and also you can use Internet based venues to sell works of art, and identify styles, mediums, and marks.

Many works of art are identified by going to the Internet and reading something related to a word , phrase or name on a work of art, or on the back or sides of a work of art, it is great inexpensive research source for you art dealer business!

Constructivism

The Constructivism movement was between 1919 and 1934 and Constructivism was a creation of the Russian avant-garde.

Some Artists of Constructivism

Altman, Natan $30,000

Berlewi, Henryk $11,000

Buchholz, Erich $33,000

Calderara, Antonio $7500

Dexel, Walter$65,000

Gabo, Naum $200,000

Kassak, Lajos $15,000

Kobro, Katarzyna $25,000

Lissitzky, El $550,000

Malevich, Kasimir $17,000,000

Martin, Kenneth $3500

Top Secret Technique 83
You do not need to be a PhD graduate to succeed in your own art business

You do not need to be a doctor of philosophy, a graduate or even that educated in anything but art, to succeed in your own art dealer business. Actually if you are a good sales person or good with talking with people you can be a great a great art dealer.

It is good to be a good manager, and you should have resources available to you like internet connection, a computer, a place to store your works of art. But mainly all you need is art to sell and a way to show these works of art to customers that might want to purchase those works of art. Then most all the top secret techniques shown in this book can be used very well!

Some All Movements Women artists

Ghada Amer $225,415

Diane Arbus $552,600

Lynda Benglis $167,300

Rosa Bonheur $491,000

Lee Bontecou $1,900,000

Cecily Brown $1,600,000

Niki de Saint Phalle $1,136,000

Sonia Delaunay $3,900,000

Tracey Emin $247,000

Marisol Escobar $912,000

Helen Frankenthaler $800,000

Katharina Fritsch $282,000

Ellen Gallagher $668,000

Top Secret Technique 84
To succeed, in art dealing you must be willing to ask questions, remain curious, and open to new knowledge

Part of being a great art dealer is in the aggregation of information about works of art. Even opinions from other people that own works of art can be helpful as sometimes their great grandfather might have purchased the work of art and by asking questions you can get valuable information about the work of art. You have to be a very good art dealer detective and read between the lines of what people say, and get to the reality of what most people say about art.

Always remain curious about art, and always ask the obvious questions as well as the most obscure questions:

1. Where did this come from?
2. When did you get it?
3. Who did you get this art from?
4. How was this art created?
5. What is the name I see here?
6. What is this mark?
7. Why did you buy this?

8. Why are you selling this now?

9. Do you have any other pictures?

10. Do you have the receipt for the art?

11. Are you an artist?

All of these questions could get you information and into better deals, and can help you in your research on works of art in your art dealer adventures!

Top Secret Technique 85
Like a Samurai in the beginning, you might fall down 7 times, but get up 8!

When you try to research, sell buy and other aspects of being an art dealer you will make mistakes. This is considered falling down like written in the Hagakure which is way of the samurai, and it was written by the Japanese for his highest level samurai. It describes how a samurai should act in the community and world. One of the phrases written there in the Hagakure is for a samurai to fall down 7 times and get up 8, this was meant to inspire the thought that if you fail 7 times in what you want to achieve then you need to get up again and fight for what you want.

This applies to being an art dealer, it is imperative that when you make mistakes in art buying, selling, or research you should always take it as a learning experience and then get back up and on to the next adventure in art dealing. Remember every experience is a learning experience, even if the lesson learned was a good one or a bad one, even the one where you just sold a million dollar work of art for only $20,000!

Top Secret Technique 86 Anyone can do this, You are the product of your own choosing

No matter what your field of expertise is from a janitor, to a scientist, anyone can be a weekend art dealer. It is a great profession, as it requires only a small amount of time, and you can do it as much as you like, or as little as you like. You can set limits to the hours you want to work on research, sales, buying and meeting people at antique stores, markets, shows, or representing new artists.

It's all about buying and selling so you can work at your own speed. Some successful part time weekend art dealers that I have met have only sold a painting every month or so, and they spend an hour every week looking for art.

It can add to your income in a hobby fun way, but if you wanted to you could do it for more income whenever you need additional income. It's a great self employed small business to get into!

Top Secret Technique 87 Adventure is there, waiting for you every weekend

In my travels around the country I have found that the art is there waiting for you every weekend. Even if it rains or snows there are indoor markets in every town, and when its not raining the outdoor markets are great for art hunting. And if you can not find these low end markets then there is always galleries, antique stores, and tag sales, garage sales, and yard sales to wet your art appetite. An adventure awaits you every weekend of the year out there!

Top Secret Technique 88 Making a Profit, Not a Living in your Art Dealer Business

When you are pricing your art works always remember to make a profit not a living in your art dealer business. The living will come along soon enough. But understand that this is a part time venture, and you should have fun with it. Try to buy under priced works of art and sell them for what they are worth. Never ask more than what the art is worth unless you want to sit on it for a long time.

Selling and placing art is the number one aspect of being an art dealer, also the excitement of learning about every work of art and the artist that created it, makes you one work of art smarter, as you go along.

Being an art dealer is a learning process, and each art deal you are involved in, increases your art dealer network of people and art knowledge. If I told you that I was still learning about art every day, you would not believe it but it is true!

Top Secret Technique 89
Learn from the mistakes of others, and sometimes yours!

As you trade, sell and buy art part of the fun is meeting and socializing with other art dealers, and antique dealers. There is never a time when dealers get together that they cannot resist telling the story of the one that got away, the one that sold for a fortune, or the technique, secret that they have used to make a deal, sell something or buy something.

Most of the learning that you will get out there in the art dealing world comes from experiences gained in the actual adventure of dealing and meeting your peers out there. You should learn from all these other people, and make sure you do not make the same mistakes, but definitely use the good techniques that they advise, as they are a great group of people always trying to help each other out.

Also it's good to talk with these colleagues as they will help you with your problems in research, they might even get you into their research channels, and maybe even collaborate on some deals with you.

Top Secret Technique 90 Knowing the who, what, where and why of the average art customer

Who will buy your art?

1. Art Collectors

2. Art Experts

3. High-end Art Experts

4. Middle just starting to Learning Expert

5. The Regular People

Depending on the nature of your show space, website or gallery your customers are likely to be predominantly members of the public, though you may also have some business clients.

Members of the public might include:

1. People that see your website

2. People walking by and tourists

3. Art enthusiasts, including artists, art critics, collectors, dealers, and experts, etc.
4. Art students and young people

Your corporate clients may include:

1. Business people that see your website
2. Other galleries, dealers
3. Professional interior designers
4. Businesses that purchase art to decorate their own premises
5. Businesses that maintain an art collection

These kinds of groups of buyers are your main marketing areas so focus on knowing who you are selling to, and this will lead you to success in your art dealing adventures!

Top Secret Technique 91
Never lose sight of your end goal or your dream of art treasure

Always set goals for what you want to get out of your art dealer business.

Some people want just to make a lot of money, but others want to make some money but meet people and be around exciting artists and their associates.

The dream of finding an art treasure can be a compelling one. All art dealers that have been doing this for a while have the story of the one art treasure that they found.

And if you are lucky there were many art treasures along the way.

But in the end, when an art treasure is found whether it be a $10,000 dollar art work or a $1,000,000 art work the most important thing is that you did it, and you saved a work of art from being thrown out or destroyed.

Also you are serving a need of people, as they will begin to trust in your judgment of art, as some investors will be asking you what art will be appreciating in value.

And when you get to that level it is the ultimate reward!

Top Secret Technique 92
If it were easy to find a Picasso, everybody would be rich! But, it happens, more than you think!

Yes, Picasso works of art are out there every day you have to understand the artist, and look at his catalog raisonne, and you will see that many works of art created by Picasso were sold at museum stores in Spain to many tourists.

There are many prints, etchings, and graphics, and ceramics all out there to be discovered.

You need an art signature book like The Art Signature File on Kindle as it has many art signatures of Picasso to identify these works of art, as he signed many different ways.

As a matter of fact a friend of mine was able to buy a ceramic in a thrift store once, for $150 that was a Picasso ceramic, and was able to immediately sell it to a gallery for $6500!

And that was at a time when they used to say, that no Picasso works of art could be found because his works of art were selling at auction for millions of dollars!

Top Secret Technique 93
Are You Crazy? You Can't Make Money Doing That!

Most people would think that you could not make money being an art dealer on the weekend.

This is not a true statement, if you know what you are looking for, know how to buy it at the right price, and can sell it at a better price then you can make money doing this, and become an art dealer.

The difference between Madison Avenue art dealers and you is only the size of the deals, but do not diminish the value of the small deal. Woolworths made a fortune selling 5 and 10 cent items, and buying a $20 painting and selling it for $200 is no different.

It's all about you, and using the techniques that are included in this book, along with a great network of other dealers, experts, artisans, and craftsmen. You can do it, anyone can do it!

Top Secret Technique 94 Survival in the Weekend Art Dealer world is dependent upon your perseverance

Perseverance in the art dealing business is a very important trait, even though you are doing this on the weekend, you should always keep some sort of regular schedule for finding new works of art. You should also have a backup plan of places to go even on line for say an hour every weekend, to get inventory for your art dealer business.

Some More Women Artists

Artemisia Gentileschi $658,000

Isa Genzken $314,500

Nan Goldin $284,500

Mary Heilmann $182,500

Barbara Hepworth $2,600,000

Eva Hesse $4,500,000

Hannah Hoch $824,000

Jenny Holzer $881,000

Bharti Kher $1,500,000

Kathe Kollwitz $299,000

Top Secret Technique 95 Decide now that you can start an art business that you'll enjoy!

Do not wait, if you have an interest in art, and you have an interest in being an art dealer, and then do it now. Do not procrastinate, as it does not take a lot of money to do this business.

You can start this business by getting a price guide and signature book like the Art Signature File on kindle or ipad, which is very inexpensive, and Kindle from amazon is inexpensive, or you can get Kindle for your PC or lap top and then just start going on line, and visiting local flea markets, yard sales, garage sales, estate sales etc.

Start out small and get a feel for what you are doing. It will be an enjoyable adventure, and hey you never know what you will do! Your first deal might be amazing, but trust me when you make your first deal that is a magical moment that will never go away. And you can now call yourself an art dealer as that is what you are!

Top Secret Technique 96 Getting married to an art research project and sticking, with it too long

Sometimes the time it takes to research a work of art can be costly and cost a lot of time money. And time money for a part time art dealer, should be spent wisely. You should always delegate your time for your art research projects. Remember that if you waste too much time researching works of art, you will have no time left for the business of being an art dealer.

I have personally spent years on research of certain works of art, as I felt they were very important works of art. But I always made sure that the time was split modestly between the deals that needed to be made, and the sales that needed to be accomplished.

Yes it is difficult especially when you have something that deep down you know is important. You can actually have taken it to many experts that were not sure of the work of art also. And they in my case knew it was a very good work of art, but just could not figure it out.

So as this research project was to help a friend, and I knew that the friend would cut me in on the deal at the end, I spent much longer than I normally do to research works of art. We even did very expensive infrared reflectography by a very famous museum conservator on these 2 works of art on paper. In the end the conservator also agreed that the artist was a master painter, as he could see in the under drawing, beneath the paint that the sketches were very accomplished.

I in the end moved to a different town, and briefly kept up with my friend, so they I suppose are still there to be discovered someday by someone.

Just remember that "out of chaos comes opportunity", and in this case, I developed an inexpensive way to do infrared reflectography using a simple video camera, and an infrared filter, that I now use very often for no charge but my time in art research! Learn to turn bad ones into good ones, as also I learned about the avante garde synchronism and futurism styles of art, and really became an expert in that area because of this research that took me into the back rooms of many museums, and galleries during this time!

Top Secret Technique 97
The Secret, of Making Money, with Your Small Business is Simple!

The secret to making money in the business of art dealing is to keep your art inventory churning, with art being sold, or marketed on line, and on consignment in many antique, and flea market dealer booths or stores around your town. Also another secret is you are what you have bought. Some dealers that I have known use this simple rule for their businesses; if they are not buying they are not making any money.

If you have the channels setup for selling well then you will always be looking for inventory to sell. Every dollar you spend should bring you in 2 to 5 dollars in sales. So if you are not buying, you will not be making any money. A great way to buy art is to advertise that you buy art. Another dealer I know always had an ad running in the local newspapers, bulletin boards, and advertising areas. And he would get so many works of art from people who never had a garage sale, yard sale, or public sale. Some people just never do public sales, and they have art from many years ago stored in their basements and attics, and they want to get rid of them, or they want to raise money.

If these people want too much money for their art then you can play the consignment contract where you will pay them what they want if you can sell it for the amount they want, and they will give you a commission. So the secret to making money in the art dealer business is to have art to sell. Buying and selling that is the business of the art dealer, and it is a simple fact!

Top Secret Technique 98
Show it off to your network!

Sometimes you just do not know what to do with art items you buy. Especially if you are new to art buying and you buy some mistakes.

The first thing to do is show it to your network of antique dealers, art dealers, friends, family etc. of course some of the network who are experts might laugh, but they will probably have good input information for you to learn from.

Your informal friends and family might see what you saw in the work of art, and offer to buy it at the price you bought at, or for a little profit or you can give it as a gift.

Your antique dealers might even put it in their store on consignment, as some antique stores are now selling contemporary works, as their customers are sometimes looking for those things.

Also your network flea market dealers will take consignments also.

Some More Women Artists

Lee Krasner $3,170,000

Louise Elizabeth Vigee Lebrun $792,000

Sherrie Levine $713,000

Lee Lozano $602,500

Sarah Lucas $141,250

Agnes Martin $4,700,000

Julie Mehretu $2,300,000

Beatriz Milhazes $1,200,000

Elizabeth Murray $132,000

Alice Neel $1,650,000

Louise Nevelson $634,000

Elizabeth Peyton $856,000

Jenny Saville $2,400,000

Cindy Sherman $3,900,000

Kiki Smith $295,000

Pat Steir $80,000

Irma Stern $4,900,000

Elaine Sturtevant $710,000

Dorothea Tanning $104,000

Rosemarie Trockel $962,500

Anne Truitt $54,000

Suzanne Valadon $218,000

Rachel Whiteread $887,305

Sue Williams $96,000

Lisa Yuskavage $1,400,000

Top Secret Technique 99
Set realistic goals for your Art adventures

One weekend art dealer I know, when she is out running errands, or traveling and about always keeps the art search going. She always works towards the goal of finding at least one work of art that can be marketed, or collected on each of her trips. She will actually include flea markets, antique stores, and local thrift sales in her trips, always dropping by to see if anything new has stumbled in. Many days she finds nothing, but sooner or later she will actually find something. Also she sets up a regular schedule for pick ups from some organizations that get donations. I think her attainable goals may be as vast as every week she wants to find something, that can be marketed or collected.

Current Record Prices of Art at Auction

Agasse Jacques Laurent $5,800,000

Aivazovsky Ivan $3,138,461

Albers Josef $1,136,000

Alma-Tadema Sir Lawrence $2,800,000

Andre Carl $2,032,000

Archipenko Alexander $2,667,408

Arellano Juan $1,102,500

Arp Jean $2,800,000

Ast Balthasar van der $2,800,000

Avercamp Hendrick $8,688,000

Bacon Francis $27,598,245

Bakst Lev Samolovich $1,215,552

Balla Giacomo $4,400,000

Balthus Jean Balthasar Klossowski $6,736,000

Baraud Jean $1,200,000

Barcelo Miquel $1,574,683

Barocci Fredrico $2,600,000

Barry James $1,819,259

Bartolommeo Fra Baccio della Porta $9,750,000

Top Secret Technique 100 Traps and mistakes to avoid!

You should know these art dealer traps and mistakes to avoid so that you do not invest your hard earned money in the wrong places when it comes to buying selling and trading art.

1. Always be careful of the person that tries to over sell you on buying a work of art.

2. If the artwork smells freshly painted or looks just created be careful it might be a fake, unless its a contemporary artist.

3. If another art dealer tries to sell you something that is too good to be true, it might have been checked out, and it might have something wrong with it, like major restoration, or it might be a stolen work of art or part of a divorce distribution, with problems in its legal ability to be sold.

Even though I know a weekend art dealer who bought from another art dealer a Hiroshige woodblock print for $5000 and they both knew that it was valuable. And later on that night the art dealer that sold it, researched it better, and discovered it was worth $100,000 and he pounded on the art dealer friend of his, and demanded that there be some settlement. The other art dealer then said ok, so what ever it sells for over the $5000 I gave you then we will split the profit 50/50? And they were able to settle it in a friendly way. But these things happen; sometimes not all art dealers know everything!

Top Secret Technique 101 Strategies and techniques to help you in bad economic times!

You should always have works of art up for sale in public on line venues, like ebay, ebid and others, even though you are selling privately from your home, or your gallery. These sales will help you get through trying times in your art dealing business. Also these venues are great for getting rid of stored inventory as you acquire many works of art along the way.

You do not need to get a very large profit from your artworks; you can even just sell them for double what you paid for the art. You will never go wrong as long as you are a good buyer of art and you get the works for the right price. That is the name of this art dealer game, you must know what you are buying, unless it's an inexpensive work of art, and then it's OK to take the risk.

Current Record Prices of Art at Auction

Baselitz George $1,100,000

Basquiat Jean-Michel $5,509,500

Bazille Jean-Frederic $5,328,000

Beckman Max $22,560,000

Beert Osias $1,825,000

Beihong Xu $6,925,449

Bellotto Bernardo called Il Canaletto Younger $5,642,000

Bellows George Wesley $27,502,500

Benson Frank Weston $1,821,000

Benton Thomas Hart $1,808,000

Beuckelaer Joachim $3,909,600

Bierstadt Albert $6,400,000

Blake William $3,928,000

Blakelock Ralph Albert $3,525,750

Top Secret Technique 102
Do not think a million-dollar painting will NOT be discovered for $50 on Ebay, Ebid or other online auctions!

Some people think that Ebay is a place where fakes and not real paintings and works of art are being sold. This is true in some instances, but believe it or not there are sleepers to be found there also. One weekend art dealer buys sculpture and bronzes there, and then sells them at Sotheby's for great rewards.

Another weekend art dealer has purchased art works for thousands and tripled his investment immediately after his receiving of the item. Interior decorators also have discovered sleepers there also.

More Art Records

Caravaggio aka Merisi Michelangelo $1,000,000

Carlevarijs Luca $2,000,000

Carracci Lodovico $13,703,703

Carracci Annibale $5,227,500

Cassatt Mary $4,072,500

Castiglione Giuseppe $2,291,500

Cattelan Maurizio $1,850,000

Ceruti Giacomo $1,642,012

Cezanne Paul $60,500,000

Chadwick Lynn $1,860,000

Chagall Marc $13,500,000

Chamberlain Jonh $1,024,000

Chardin Jean-Baptiste Simeon $2,400,000

Chase William Merritt $10,000,000

Chasseriau Theodore $1,029,840

Chillida Eduardo $3,748,148

Top Secret Technique 103
Take an aspiring artist whose work you admire to dinner!

Being a weekend part time art dealer, you might have dry periods where you will have to work at being a true art dealer. So, most all art dealers have artists that they are friendly to and help along the way. You should pursue these relationships, and take an artist friend to dinner. Buy their works for your own collection and make an agreement with them to deal their art.

You can then take their art on consignment in your home art gallery, and when you have those dinners for your art customers, you can maybe sell a few during slow times. This will help your aspiring artist while benefiting you in commissions, and the more of the aspiring artist's works that are out there the more your own "best" collection will appreciate!

More Art Records

De Kooning Willem $63,500,000

De Chirico Georgio $7,175,500

De Nittis Giuseppe $1,500,000

De Stael Nicolas $1,500,000

Degas Edgar $28,000,000

Del Sarto Andrea $11,395,000

Del Piombo Sebastiano $1,200,000

Delacroix Eugene $7,750,000

Delaunay Robert $5,170,000

Delvaux Paul $4,500,000

Derain Andre $6,848,000

Deutsch Ludwig $1,674,074

Dewing Maria Oakley $2,020,000

Diebenkorn Richard $6,176,000

Dix Otto $5,400,000

Doig Peter $1,547,169

Domenichino $3,000,000

Top Secret Technique 104
How to set up your weekend part time art dealer's art gallery in your home!

You need to set up a gallery in your home for potential customers. Most people do not like to have businesses run out of their home. They think that being a weekend part time art dealer is a trivial thing and selling art off your wall is embarrassing. Actually if you set up your business right and have business cards, and letterheads and all the business requirements, this is not such a trivial thing.

You see if one is an art dealer, one should be confident in what one does. Dealing under these conditions can, actually enhance the environment for this activity. Imagine a collector drops by with invitation you have a conversational dinner a glass of brandy and then you retire to the gallery living room, study etc.

Here you tell your stories of your new acquisitions or the promising new artist you are representing. The collector then decides or views for a decision on the works you have in a restful and friendly environment. Believe it or not most exclusive fine art galleries in New York City, have setups similar with rents in the $20,000 to $100,000 a month area! I know of one gallery where I went to a person to sell a painting and he had his gallery in his home. You walked in and there was a $1,000,000 Picasso on an easel and to the left was a beautiful comfortable couch, and a library shelf of art books. He had a nice glass table I opened my portfolio and showed him my artwork. His assistant came in and asked if I would like a coffee or tea, and we then talked about the artist's career and his works.

You should always have a composition book that is setup as your art dealer's research book, where you can add photos, and information about works of art, like signatures you find on particular works of art, and monograms that you are checking out and researching. Here you should have notes on front, edge, back conditions, age along with images of all these views.

Shortly after we made a deal for a nice 5 figure price and I thought of him no the less for having his business in the heart of the finest neighborhood in Manhattan in his home.

The main thing important to being a weekend art dealer is the knowledge of your expertise. It is a purely academic type of business where your buyer is knowledgeable and you should be somewhat knowledgeable about the works you represent.

Art appreciation is a wonderful acquired taste. It is taught to many college novices in their first years of education. It is important for it represents the things made by man. But even the uneducated being has the human ability to appreciate and more importantly create art. There are many libraries and places for us to learn, so being college educated is not a prerequisite to being a weekend part time art dealer!

More Art Records

Falk Robert Rafellovich $1,800,000

Fantin-Latour Henri $10,000,000

Farny Henry $1,212,500

Fautrier Jean $2,500,000

Feininger Lyonel $7,688,888

Figino Giovanni Ambrogio $1,400,000

Filonov Pavel Nikolaevich $1,760,992

Fischl Eric $1,920,000

Flanagan Barry $1,177,358

Fonatna Lucio $4,030,188

Foujita Tsuguharu $5,000,000

Fragonard Jean-Honore $8,000,000

Francis Sam Samuel Lewis $4,048,000

Francken Frans II $1,205,250

Freud Lucien $33,600,000

Friedrich Casper David $1,000,000

Frieseke Frederick C. $2,368,000

Top Secret Technique 105 The Museum Curator can sometimes be your Best Friend!

Sometimes when the weekend art dealer is researching art, the museum curator can be a very helpful person to consult. They know their collections well and are very learned in the study of art. Even though one might think them to be like the president of a business at the top of the positions in the museum, they are very approachable.

First off they are very busy people so respect any time they will give you and do not waste their time. Second usually if they can not help you with your particular art research project they will lead you in the right direction. When researching art always try to pick the curator with the museum that has art that is similar to the art you are researching. This technique will give you the most rewarding results.

The curator can be a useful consultant during your art research adventures. They have special information in to the provenance and can sometimes solve mysteries with a different perspective as they have vested interests in their collections.

Also the curators have and important list of people they have connections with so they can refer you to many people and institutions that can help you along the way. So for those important projects, where you need help, along the way try giving the curator a try!

Sensational Art Sales

Goltzius Hendrick $1,500,000

Gontcharova Natalia $10,900,000

Gonzalez Julio $3,419,500

Gonzalez-Torres Felix $1,500,000

Gorky Arshile-V. $3,962,500

Gossaert Jan called Mabuse $1,652,500

Goya y Lucientes Francisco J. $7,020,000

Goyen Jan Van $1,875,765

Grigoriev Boris Dimitrievich $1,846,153

Gris Juan $8,479,500

Gros Baron Jean Antonie $2,346,775

Guanzhong Wu $1,194,960

Guardi Francesco $13,943,200

Top Secret Technique 106 Always remember...there are 4 reasons successful art dealers do what they do

1. An art dealer buys things and sells things.(Such as buying art and reselling it for a higher price, the most profitable thing)

2. An art dealer gets things for FREE and sells things. (Such as taking works on consignment, selling artists works given to them to sell, representing new artists, or artists estates for a percentage of the sale price)

3. An Art Dealer creates and makes markets for new upcoming artists that want to say something in a creative way in their art. (Usually for a percentage of the market made, which can be the most profitable, of all 4 reasons, some successful art dealer examples would be Mary Boone, Leo Castelli)

4. An Art Dealer places art into places where it will be kept for many years to come, and can be a held example of human accomplishment! (This just goes with the profession, and is a perk for this business)

Look at These Art Prices!

Hals Franz $12,350,000

Hals Dirk $1,047,500

Hamen Juan van der $1,158,997

Hammershoi Vilhelm $1,093,333

Harris Lawren $2,200,000

Hartley Marsden $1,652,500

Hassam Frederick Childe $20,000,000

Heade Martin Johnson $2,760,000

Heckel Erich $1,758,440

Heda William Claesz $1,430,000

Heem Jan Davidz de $6,000,000

Top Secret Technique 107
Art Discoveries will be here for a while

Sometimes a Weekend Art Dealer will go through a dry spell, and think that all the art that is to be discovered, has been discovered. This is a negative assumption, and the fact is the smart and industrious art dealer will always discover art. One art dealer I know was having a dry spell, no matter, what technique he used, he could not find anything. So he did OK dealing newer modern works from his artist base, he represented. But that was not nearly as exciting as the discovery and identification of an unfounded work of art. During this time on the weekends, it just did not seem to be profitable to search the usual places for art. So he went to a friend's yard sale at the end of the day, around 3 PM. He had a slice of pizza and talked of his finds and discoveries of the past, his friend was a successful weekend art dealer also, so he had some great tales to add to the discussion.

As they were talking a customer picked up a lamp and then my friend started looking around at the sale while his friend helped the customer. As he was looking at the pictures and works of art that was there he noticed a well-painted landscape of a burrow in a mountain area. When his friend was finished with his customer, he asked him about the painting.

The friend said, "it's just a landscape" for you, "you can have it for $100". The painting had a signature on the back, so the weekend dealer said, "I think this could be a good painting"! His friend said "check it out, and if it is good I will split the profit with you"! The dealer went to his library and researched the artist, and discovered it was listed and the signature matched a signature in the Art Signature File.

He rushed back and told the friend that he should not sell it at his yard sale! To make a long story short, they sold the painting at auction and got $2,900, a nice profit for a Saturday afternoon!

Now the dealer's friend has asked him to look at all his paintings, to discover another one! Imagine every art dealer, antiques dealer, and Ebay dealer had been to this guy's sale that morning and afternoon, (at least 350 people) and not one, had the eye to see that this work could be valuable!

Top Secret Technique 108
The Good Art Gallery or The
Bad Art Gallery

In the world we are always experiencing the good and the bad in everything we do. So it makes sense that there are good art galleries and bad art galleries. From the art collector or customer perspective, these galleries might be all "Good", but I think that if an art gallery uses tricky techniques for buying their art inventory, then they probably use the same tricky techniques on the sell side of the equation.

The "Good" art gallery does not waste the time of the weekend art dealer, they assist them and respect the idea that they keep them in mind when they will occasionally try to sell them something. The "Good" art gallery tries to be fair in the pricing of the art, and does not excessively use their connections to take advantage of the weekend art dealer.

The "Good" art gallery is also helpful if they feel they cannot sell the artwork being offered, and will actually guide you on a path to another gallery or even collector for your sale.

The "Bad" art gallery won't invite you into their office, and feel they are better than you, they feel you are a provincial hay seed and you feel like it after you meet with them if you are lucky! The "Bad" art gallery, wastes your time by giving you a "high" estimate over the phone after seeing pictures, then after your travel to them and the artwork is in their hand, they change the estimate or the terms of purchase to their advantage. The "Bad" art gallery usually will talk down the art before you even open your wrapped artwork. Be careful with these art galleries!

The key is to walk before they make you feel that you have a very low priced artwork. Psychologically the "Bad" art gallery can lower your already identified idea of what you know your artwork is worth. If the art gallery person has not even seen your artwork, and he is talking it down, DO NOT leave it with him!

These kinds of art gallery directors will ask you to leave the artwork with them for 3 months; they will then say they will get you a high price for the art. Then they will call you at the very end of the time and say they have an offer for 1/3 to ½ less than that high price they estimated. In the end they get 20% off you and you get half of what you could have gotten on your own, with an ad in the newspaper!

There is no room for cheap art gallery directors. These people should be used car dealers, but somehow they get into the position of being associated with major famous art galleries, probably because they were born into the families of the art business.

In example I know a weekend art dealer who told me the story of how they went to the highest rated American art gallery in New York City, and had this time wasting experience.

Fortunately, on the way out of this gallery, our weekend art dealer went into the gallery next door to this highly overrated art gallery, and met the nicest director, who was familiar with that art gallery director and his dubious techniques.

Because of the nature of art and its value, some art gallery directors feel that they are the royalty, and have forgotten that they are simply salesmen with knowledge of art customers and their product "art".

The Opportunities Are There For You!

Indenbaum Leon $4,627,854

Ingres Jean-Auguste Dominique $2,000,000

Jawlensky Alex von $8,296,000

Johns Jasper $80,000,000

Joli de Dipi Antonio $1,200,000

Jordaens Jacob $3,300,000

Jorn Asgar $2,099,500

Judd Donald $4,629,500

Kahlo Frida $5,616,000

Kandinsky Wassily $40,000,000

Kane Paul $3,300,000

Kapoor Anish $2,256,000

Kelly Mike $2,704,000

Top Secret Technique 109
Art prices are like stock prices they, go up and they go down

In the stock market a stock can be watched on a daily basis and its price will fluctuate up and down during the day. Some stocks go up and down over a yearly period in a cyclical pattern. Fine Art is very much similar in its cyclical patterns, but it's much more stable in its investment performance. Certain works of art have a period of exceptional appreciation, and then for some reason they fall out of grace with the collector or investor.

Art can be a great investment if you purchase the right artists works at the right time. There was a time when the works of art by Andy Warhol were selling in the millions then they went through a price drop, and then they increased in value.

But if you look at his sales records at auction in the next 10 to 20 years they will definitely be higher in price as time goes by.

That is the great aspect of collecting investment grade fine art; it is one of the most stable investments one can make. One reason for this fact is that unlike the stock market where a stock can be created to an unlimited amount, the fine artist can only create so much art in their lifetime!

So only so much original artwork can be there to be acquired, which alternately affects the price of art. This makes artworks more and more valuable as time goes by! Of course, knowing when to buy and sell is the key to being a successful marketer of fine art.

Top Secret Technique 110
Socialize with artists

Believe it or not you can actually socialize with many older well known artists, and most all contemporary artists. In my travels I and many of my colleagues have been very fortunate in meeting many famous artists, and actually becoming friends with them, and have been invited to many an artist's studio, where you can actually see their works of art being created.

Once I was invited to talk with an artist who I had a work of art I was researching, and when I went into his second floor studio, that was part of his apartment, there was a hall with very valuable original Paul Klee drawings and art, and on the way to the studio, in a room was a Picasso oil painting that had never been seen!

In his studio he would paint street people, and he would go down stairs, and hand a card to people walking by, and then would pay them $10 to sit for him and he would paint them. He had been doing this technique since the 1940's and he was about 84 years old at this time that I was in his studio.

These opportunities come about quite a bit, and the real art dealer, instigates these things whenever possible. Especially with young up and moving artists, it's a good idea to pick an artist that you like and make a request to visit their studio, and make a deal to market their art. And try to get exclusive deals, if anything you can later on maybe sell the contract to a larger art dealer, or group for a profit.

You never know, you could one day become a Leo Castelli, or a Mary Boone who had the eye for contemporary artists and made a fortune, in his judgments of who would someday become wanted by all the world's collectors!

Top Secret Technique 111
Art is a conversation creator

If you aspire to be a weekend art dealer, you must understand a simple secret of art. Art is a conversation creator, and you can demonstrate this statement by the fact that nobody can look at a work of art and not say something about it.

We as humans must express ourselves creatively and when we view a work created by another human being we must say something about it. Also to most people in the world art is a foolish thing that has no significance in the average person's life.

But still being a human when observing the art we must say something. Now when you have a work of art that you in your weekend art dealer business can not really identify, then you MUST put it on your wall and invite people over and let them view it. This is a secret technique that I have personally been amazed by.

Believe it or not from the mouth of babes can come genius, and many a work of art has been identified listening to the conversations of the masses viewing art!

More Sales Records

Kirchner Ernst Ludwig $38,100,000

Klee Paul $7,000,000

Klein Yves $4,720,000

Klimt Gustav $135,000,000

Kline Franz $6,400,000

Koekkoek Barend Cornelis $1,736,706

Kokoschka Oskar $2,700,000

Koons Jeff $25,800,000

Korovin Konstantin $1,696,000

Krasner Lee $3,170,000

Kustodiev Boris $2,900,000

Lam Wifredo $1,322,500

Lane Fritz Hugh $5,500,000

Laurencin Marie $1,300,000

Laurens Henri $1,472,000

Lavery John $1,983,240

Lawrence Sir Thomas $4,000,000

Art Galleries that buy and sell works of art

Also a gallery label can help in the research of provenance, and value, plus sometimes a gallery will buy it back, at higher value. You just have to make an appointment, and drop by or send an image of the work of art and they will let you know if they want to buy the art back from you.

A La Vielle Russie

A. Jain Marunouchi

Acquavella Galleries, Inc.

Adam Baumgold Gallery

Adamo Gallery

Adelson Galleries

Adler & Conkright Fine Art

Aicon Gallery

Alexandre Gallery

Algus Greenspon

Allan Stone Gallery

Amador Gallery

American Illustrators Gallery

Ameringer | McEnery | Yohe

Ana Tzarev Gallery

Anita Shapolsky Gallery

Arcadia Fine Arts, Inc.

Babcock Galleries

Barbara Mathes Gallery

Bernarducci Meisel Gallery

Berry-Hill Galleries

Berwald Oriental Art

Bill Hodges Gallery

Bonni Benrubi Gallery

Brian Riley1Projects

Brooke Alexander Gallery

Carlton Rochell Asian Art

Carolina Nitsch

Cecilia de Torres

Chaib-Sedduk Contemporary Art

CharlElie Artspace

Christina Ray

Contemporary African Art Gallery

D. Wigmore Fine Art

Daphne Alazraki Fine Art

David Findlay Galleries

David Findlay Jr. Fine Art

David Tunick, Inc.

Davidson Contemporary

Diane Villani Editions

Didier Aaron, Inc.

Edward Tyler Nahem Fine Art

Edwynn Houk Gallery

Ethan Cohen Fine Arts

Forum Gallery

Fountain Gallery

Francis M. Naumann Fine Art

Franklin Parrasch Gallery

Frederico Seve Gallery

Gagosian Gallery

Galerie St. Etiennel

Gallery SAKIKO New York

Gavin Brown's enterprise

Gerald Peters Gallery

Gering & Lopez Gallery

Gitterman Gallery

Godel & Co.

Goedhuis Contemporary

GP Deva Frontier Art & X-Power Gallery

Greenberg Van Doren Gallery

Hammer Galleries

Hammer Graphics

Heller Gallery

Helly Nahmad Gallery

Heskin Contemporary

Higher Pictures

Higher Pictures

Hirschl & Adler Galleries

Hollis Taggart Galleries

Howard Greenberg Gallery

IR77 Contemporary Art

Island Weiss Gallery

Isselbacher Gallery

J.N. Bartfield Galleries

Jacobson Howard Gallery

Jadite Galleries

James Goodman Gallery

Jan Krugier Gallery

Jane Kahan Gallery

Janet Borden Inc.

Jason McCoy, Inc.

June Kelly Gallery

KANSAS

Kate Werble Gallery

Katharina Rich Perlow Gallery

Keith De Lellis Gallery

Kennedy Galleries

Knoedler & Company

Kouros Gallery

KS Art / Kerry Schuss

L&M Arts

Laurence Miller Gallery

Lawrence Steigrad Fine Arts

Leo Castelli Gallery

Leo Kaplan Ltd.

Leo Kesting Gallery

Leonard Hutton Galleries

Leslie Feely Fine Art

Lillian Heidenberg Fine Art

Louis K. Meisel Gallery

Lumen Gallery

Maccarone

Manhattan Art & Antiques Center

Margarete Roeder Gallery

Marian Goodman Gallery

Marianne Boesky Gallery

Marlborough Gallery

Martin Lawrence Galleries

Mary Boone Gallery

Mary-Anne Martin Fine Art

Maxwell Davidson Gallery

McCaffrey Fine Art

McKee Gallery

McKee Gallery

Michael Rosenfeld Gallery

Michael Werner Gallery

Michail & Lombardo Gallery

Mimi Ferzt Gallery

Mireille Mosler Ltd.

Mitchell-Innes & Nash Gallery

Moeller Fine Art Ltd.

OK Harris

Peter Blum Gallery

Phoenix Ancient Art S.A.

Renwick Gallery

Richard L. Feigen & Co.

Robin Rice Gallery

Ronald Feldman Fine Arts

Roth

Salon 94

Salon 94 Bowery

Sasha Wolf Gallery

Skarstedt Gallery

SoHo Loft Gallery

Soho Photo

Spanierman Modern

Spencer Brownstone Gallery

Sperone Westwater

Staley-Wise Gallery

Stellan Holm Gallery

Susan Aberbach Fine Art

Susan Eley Fine Art

Susan Sheehan Gallery

Talwar Gallery

Team Gallery, Inc.

The Merrin Gallery

The Old Print Shop

Throckmorton Fine Art

Tibor De Nagy Gallery

Tilton Gallery

TK Asian Antiquities

Two Palms

Van de Weghe Fine Art

Wally Findlay Galleries

Ward-Nasse Gallery

Washburn Gallery

Westwood Gallery

Wharton Fine Art

White Box

White Columns

Wildenstein & Company

Zabriskie Gallery

Top Secret Technique 112
Learn all the styles of Art
Pop Art

Pop Art began during the mid-1950s, and the leading Pop artists include Andy Warhol, Robert Rauschenberg, Jasper Johns, Roy Lichtenstein, and Claes Oldenburg.

Pop Art Artists and some prices...

Adami, Valerio $17,000

Amen, Woody van $750

Arman $365,000

Artschwager, Richard $65,000

Asselbergs, Gustave $9500

Baldaccini, Cesar $60,000

Barker, Clive $2500

Bentum, Rik van $3500

Blake, Peter $20,000

Boshier, Derek $7500

Boty, Pauline

Caulfield, Patrick $20,000

d'Arcangelo, Allan $20,000

de-Guillebon, Jeanne-Claude

Dine, Jim $250,000

Donaldson, Antony $2000

Escobar, Marisol $65,000

Fahlstrom, Oyvind $100,000

Hains, Raymond $20,000

Hamilton, Richard $40,000

Hockney, David $5,407,407

Hopper, Dennis $165,282

Horkay, Istvan

Indiana, Robert $500,000

Jeong-Hwa, Choi

Johns, Jasper $80,000,000

Jones, Allen

Kanovitz, Howard $14,000

Kaufman, Steve

Kienholz, Edward $17,000

Kitaj, R B $3,000,000

Krushenick, Nicholas $3500

Laing, Gerald $1700

Lichtenstein, Roy $5,000,000

Oldenburg, Claes $2,210,000

Paolozzi, Eduardo $10,000

Phillips, Peter $17,000

Ramos, Mel $90,000

Rauschenberg, Robert $7,260,000

Richter, Gerhard $2,000,000

Rivers, Larry $450,000

Rosenquist, James $300,000

Ruscha, Edward $3,000,000

Scharf, Kenny $7000

Segal, George $600,000

Self, Colin $1500

Smith, Richard $12,000

Thiebaud, Wayne $500,000

Tilson, Joe $8000

Warhol, Andy $71,700,000

Impressionism

Impressionism movement was started in France during the mid 1860s and throughout the 1870s. The principle Impressionist painters were Pierre Auguste Renoir, Claude Monet, Paul Cézanne, Camille Pissarro, Alfred Sisley and Berthe Morisot, and Edgar Degas.

The French Impressionists

Frederic Bazille $500,000

Eugene Boudin $1,600,000

Felix Bracquemond $10,000

Marie Bracquemond $7500

Mary Cassatt $4,072,500

Gustave Caillebotte $14,300,000

Paul Cezanne $60,500,000

Gustave Colin $4700

Edgar Degas $28,000,000

Jean-Louis Forain $90,000

Paul Gauguin $40,330,000

Eva Gonzales

Armand Guillaumin $200,000

Stanislas Lepine $450,000

Edouard Manet $24,000,000

Claude Monet $80,000,000

Berthe Morisot $3,850,000

Camille Pissarro $14,601,000

Auguste Renoir $78,000,000

Emile Schuffenecker $120,000

Georges Seurat $35,200,000

Paul Signac $2,692,000

Alfred Sisley $3,000,000

Dada

Dada can be traced to the Cabaret Voltaire in Zurich in 1916, and another group was quickly organized in New York by Marcel Duchamp, movement centered at Gallery 291. The leading spirit of Dada was Marcel Duchamp.

Dada artists

Arp, Hans $450,000

Baader, Johannes $60,000

Baargeld, Johannes Theodor $30,000

Blumenfeld, Erwin $3000

Crotti, Jean $67,000

Drier, Katherine Sophie $2500

Duchamp, Marcel $1,762,500

Eggeling, Viking $30,000

Ernst, Max $2,429,500

Freytag-Loringhoven, Baroness Elsa von

Golyscheff, Jefim $23,000

Grosz, George $150,000

Hausmann, Raoul $400,000

Heartfield, John $3500

Hoch, Hannah $824,000

Huelsenbeck, Richard $1000

Janco, Marcel $40,000

Man Ray $1,504,440

Picabia, Francis $4,780,880

Prampolini, Enrico $85,000

Richter, Hans $30,000

Schad, Christian $200,000

Schamberg, Morton Livingston $280,000

Schwitters, Kurt $170,000

Stieglitz, Alfred $100,000

Taeuber-Arp, Sophie $65,000

Tschichold, Jan $1500

Van Doesburg, Theo $200,000

Van Rees, Adya

Van Rees, Otto $3500

Wood, Beatrice $8500

Abstract Expressionism

The founders of Abstract Expressionism include Hans Hofmann, Willem de Kooning, Arshile Gorky, Jackson Pollock, Mark Rothko, and Franz Kline.

Abstract Expressionism artists

Baziotes, William $300,000

Bluhm, Norman $47,000

Davie, Alan $42,000

Firestone, Robert

Francis, Sam $4,048,000

Frankenthaler, Helen $800,000

Gambini, William

Goldberg, Michael $25,000

Gorky, Arshile $3,962,500

Guston, Philip $1,835,500,000

Hartigan, Grace $10,000

Hofmann, Hans $4,297,000

Kline, Franz $6,400,000

Kooning, Elaine de $1,142,500

Kooning, Willem de $63,500,000

Krasner, Lee $3,170,000

Mitchell, Joan $9,300,000

Motherwell, Robert $7,922,500

Newell, Roy $1000

Passlof, Pat

Pollock, Jackson $140,000,000

Roos, Aart $1000

Rothko, Mark $3,000,000

Slivka, David $1000

Smith, David $400,000

Sterne, Hedda $3500

Still, Clyfford $61,000,000

Tomlin, Bradley Walker $150,000

Tworkov, Jack $70,000

Futurism

Futurism was developed in Italy around 1900. The main members of the Futurists included Carlo Carrà and Umberto Boccioni.

The Futurist's artists

Acquaviva, Giovanni $1000

Azari, Fedele

Baldessari, Iras $30,000

Baldessari, Luciano $3000

Balla, Giacomo $4,400,000

Barbieri, Osvaldo

Boccioni, Umberto $600,000

Bragaglia, Carlo

Bragaglia, Anton

Burliuk, David $55,000

Cangiullo, Francesco $28,000

Cappa, Benedetta

Carra, Carlo $350,000

Depero, Fortunato $55,000

Dottori, Gerardo $35,000

Goncharova, Natalia $10,870,500

Khlebnikov, Velimir

Kruchenykh, Alexei

Marinetti, Filippo Tommaso $15000

Matiushin, Mikhail $1500

Mayakovski, Vladimir

Munari, Bruno $5000

Popova, Liubov $1,600,000

Prampolini, Enrico $85,000

Russolo, Luigi $420,000

Sassu, Aligi $75,000

Severini, Gino $3,300,000

Sironi, Mario $450,000

Soffici, Ardengo $55,000

Wulz, Wanda

Surrealism

The French author André Breton published "The Surrealist Manifesto" in 1924. The first Surrealist exhibition took place in 1925.

Surrealism artists

Agar, Eileen $12,500

Aragon, Louis $1000

Arp, Jean $450,000

Artaud, Antonin $70,000

Ball, Hugo

Bellmer, Hans $120,000

Boiffard, Jacques Andre

Brauner, Victor $350,000

Breton, Andre $240,000

Bunuel, Luis $5000

Burliuk, David $55,000

Carrington, Leonora $360,000

Cesariny, Mario

Chirico, Giorgio de $4,800,000

Cocteau, Jean $150,000

Cornell, Joseph $400,000

Crevel, Rene $1200

Dali, Salvador $4,126,680

Delvaux, Paul $4,500,000

Desnos, Robert $10,000

Dominguez, Oscar $300,000

Donati, Enrico $16,000

Duchamp, Marcel $1,762,500

Eluard, Paul $1200

Ernst, Max $2,429,500

Evans, Dulah Marie

Gepp, Gerhard

Giacometti, Alberto $103,900,000

Hayter, Stanley William $27,000

Hugnet, Georges $2500

Kamrowski, Gerome $1000

Klee, Paul $7,000,000

Leiris, Michel

Loy, Mina $1000

Maar, Dora $14,000

Maddox, Conroy $6500

Magritte, Rene $12,700,000

Masson, Andre $400,000

Matta, Roberto $2,400,000

Mesens, E L T $2500

Miro, Joan $12,600,000

Oelze, Richard $80,000

Oppenheim, Meret $47,000

Pascali, Pino $114,000

Penrose, Roland $4000

Peret, Benjamin

Picabia, Francis $4,780,880

Seixas, Cruzeiro $1000

Styrsky, Jindrich $12,000

Tanguy, Yves $2,250,000

Art Deco

Art Deco refers generally to the decorative arts of the 1920s and 1930s a famous artist Erté, who is known as the 'father of Art Deco.'

Art Deco artists

Alen, William van

Artigas, Joan-Gardy $1000

Cappiello, Leonetto $9500

Cassandre, Adolphe Mouron $21,000

Dreyfuss, Henry

Drtikol, Frantisek $59,000

Erté Tirtoff, Romain de $35,000

Follot, Paul $1000

Lalique, Rene $55,000

Lempicka, Tamara de $8,500,000

Ragan, Leslie $11,000

Art Nouveau

The Art nouveau movement 1880's – 1905 originated in London and was also called sezessionstil in Austria, jugendstil in Germany, and modernismo in Spain.

Art Nouveau Artists

Beardsley, Aubrey $49,000

Behrens, Peter $2000

Berlage, Hendrik

de Feure, Georges $165,000

Eckmann, Otto

Endell, August

Gaudi, Antoni $15,000

Giacometti, Diego $90,000

Guimard, Hector

Horta, Victor

Klimt, Gustav $135,000,000

Klinger, Max $37,000

Lalique, Rene $55,000

Mackintosh, Charles $360,000

Mucha, Alphonse $100,000

Obrist, Hermann $1000

Riemerschmid, Richard $2500

Schiele, Egon $23,287,850

Stuck, Franz von $242,000

Thorn Prikker, Johan

Tiffany, Louis Comfort $134,000

Velde, Henry van der $9500

Vogeler, Heinrich $27,000

Wagner, Otto $5500

Blaue Reiter

The Blaue Reiter movement was from 1911 to 1914

in Germany.

Artists of the Blaue Reiter

Beckmann, Max $3,200,000

Bloch, Albert $134,000

Campendonck, Heinrich Campendonk $325,000

Jawlensky, Alexej von $8,296,000

Kandinsky, Wassily $40,000,000

Klee, Paul $7,000,000

Macke, August $3,810,040

Marc, Franz $5,061,500

Werefkin, Marianne von $24,000

Bauhaus

The Bauhaus movement was founded in Germany 1919 and continued till 1933.

Artists of the Bauhaus

Albers, Josef $1,136,000

Albers, Anni $8500

Bayer, Herbert $60,000

Behrens, Peter $2000

Bill, Max $57,000

Breuer, Marcel $2500

Citroen, Paul $25,000

Feininger, Andreas $41,000

Feininger, Lyonel $7,688,888

Feininger, T Lux $4500

Gropius, Walter $1300

Henri, Florence $4500

Itten, Johannes $25,000

Kandinsky, Wassily $40,000,000

Klee, Paul $7,000,000

Marcks, Gerhard $40,000

Mies van der Rohe, Ludwig

Moholy, Lucia

Moholy-Nagy, Laszlo $5000

Muche, Georg $93,000

Reich, Lilly

Schlemmer, Oskar $420,000

Stolzl, Gunta

Umbehr, Otto

Vordemberge-Gildewart, Friedrich $12,000

Rayonism

The Rayonism or Cubo-Futurism movement during the 1910's was the beginning of abstract art in Russia and was founded by Mikhail F. Larionov and his wife Natalia Goncharova.

Artists of the Rayonism movement

Goncharova, Natalia $10,870,500

Larionov, Mikhail $3,200,000

Cubism

The Cubism movement which included artist's who were active between 1907 and 1914, was created mainly by the painters Pablo Picasso and Georges Braque in Paris.

Artists of the Cubism movement

Adler, Jankel $104,000

Archipenko, Alexander $2,667,408

Braque, Georges $8,640,000

Delaunay, Robert $5,170,000

Duchamp-Villon, Raymond $1,762,500

Fauconnier, Henri le $45,000

Gris, Juan $8,479,500

Laurens, Henri $1,472,000

Leger, Fernand $22,407,500

Lipchitz, Jacques $1,300,000

Marcoussis, Louis $385,000

Metzinger, Jean $700.000

Picasso, Pablo $106,500,000

Rozanova, Olga $300,000

Udaltsova, Nadezhda Andreevna $20,000

Les Nabis, "The Nabis"

Nabis, which means prophet, and was created in the 1890s, by Paul Serusier and Maurice Denis.

Artists of Les Nabis

Bonnard, Pierre $8,528,000

Denis, Maurice $385,000

Maillol, Aristide $2,800,000

Serusier, Paul $400,000

Vallotton, Felix $465,000

Vuillard, Eduard $7,481,481

Vorticism

The British movement Vorticism was active between 1912 and 1915, and was a combination of Futurism and Cubism.

Artists of Vorticism

Atkinson, Lawrence $25,000

Bomberg, David $1,916,981

Dismorr, Jessica $6000

Epstein, Jacob $60,000

Gaudier Brzeska, Henri $27,000

Lewis, Wyndham $30,000

Roberts, William

Wadsworth, Edward $120,000

Post Impressionism

The Post Impressionism movement was between 1880 and 1890's.

Artists of Post Impressionism

Bonnard, Pierre $8,528,000

Cezanne, Paul $60,500,000

Dufy, Jean $100,000

Evans, Dulah Marie

Gauguin, Paul $40,330,000

Gogh, Vincent van $82,500,000

Jones, Judy

Krehbiel, Albert $1300

Matar, Joseph

Monet, Claude $80,000,000

Renoir, Pierre-Auguste $78,100,000

Rohlfs, Christian $100,000

Serusier, Paul $400,000

Signac, Paul $2,692,000

Spencer, Stanley $2,307,690

Vuillard, Eduard $7,481,481

Cobra

The Cobra art movement between 1948 and 1951 began in Denmark. Named comes from, COpenhagen, BRussels and Amsterdam. Cobra was an art movement that emulated childhood creativity and children's art styles for the purpose of expressing freedom from previous art periods.

Artists of Cobra

Alechinsky, Pierre $2,000,000

Alfelt, Else

Appel, Karel $100,000

Balle, Mogens $8500

Bille, Ejler

Brands, Eugene

Bury, Pol $27,000

Corneille Guillaume $100,000

Cox, Jan $25,000

d'Haese, Reinhoud

Diederen, Jef

Dotremont, Christian

Gaag, Lotti van der $2500

Gilbert, Stephen

Gudnason, Svavar

Heerup, Henry $10,000

Heusch, Luc de

Jacobsen, Robert $60,000

Jorn, Asger $2,099,500

Kouwenaar, Gerrit

Lindstrom, Bengt $22,000

Lucebert $50,000

Nieuwenhuijs, Jan

Nieuwenhuys, Constant

Noiret, Joseph

Ortvad, Erik $20,000

Pedersen, Carl-Henning

Rooskens, Anton $45,000

Tajiri, Shinkichi

Thommesen, Erik

Vandercam, Serge $2800

Wemaere, Pierre

Wolvecamp, Theo

Constructivism

The Constructivism movement was between 1919 and 1934 and Constructivism was a creation of the Russian avant-garde.

Artists of Constructivism

Altman, Natan $30,000

Berlewi, Henryk $11,000

Buchholz, Erich $33,000

Calderara, Antonio $7500

Dexel, Walter$65,000

Gabo, Naum $200,000

Kassak, Lajos $15,000

Kobro, Katarzyna $25,000

Lissitzky, El $550,000

Malevich, Kasimir $17,000,000

Martin, Kenneth $3500

Mashkov, Ilya $1500

Moholy-Nagy, Laszlo $5000

Pevsner, Antoine $240,000

Popova, Liubov $1,600,000

Richter, Hans $30,000

Rodchenko, Alexander $500,000

Stazewski, Henryk $4000

Stepanova, Varvara $125,000

Tatlin, Vladimir $7500

Vesnin, Alexander $30,000

All Movements Women artists

Ghada Amer $225,415

Diane Arbus $552,600

Lynda Benglis $167,300

Rosa Bonheur $491,000

Lee Bontecou $1,900,000

Cecily Brown $1,600,000

Niki de Saint Phalle $1,136,000

Sonia Delaunay $3,900,000

Tracey Emin $247,000

Marisol Escobar $912,000

Helen Frankenthaler $800,000

Katharina Fritsch $282,000

Ellen Gallagher $668,000

Artemisia Gentileschi $658,000

Isa Genzken $314,500

Nan Goldin $284,500

Mary Heilmann $182,500

Barbara Hepworth $2,600,000

Eva Hesse $4,500,000

Hannah Hoch $824,000

Jenny Holzer $881,000

Bharti Kher $1,500,000

Kathe Kollwitz $299,000

Lee Krasner $3,170,000

Louise Elizabeth Vigee Lebrun $792,000

Sherrie Levine $713,000

Lee Lozano $602,500

Sarah Lucas $141,250

Agnes Martin $4,700,000

Julie Mehretu $2,300,000

Beatriz Milhazes $1,200,000

Elizabeth Murray $132,000

Alice Neel $1,650,000

Louise Nevelson $634,000

Elizabeth Peyton $856,000

Jenny Saville $2,400,000

Cindy Sherman $3,900,000

Kiki Smith $295,000

Pat Steir $80,000

Irma Stern $4,900,000

Elaine Sturtevant $710,000

Dorothea Tanning $104,000

Rosemarie Trockel $962,500

Anne Truitt $54,000

Suzanne Valadon $218,000

Rachel Whiteread $887,305

Sue Williams $96,000

Lisa Yuskavage $1,400,000

Current Record Prices of Art at Auction

Agasse Jacques Laurent $5,800,000

Aivazovsky Ivan $3,138,461

Albers Josef $1,136,000

Alma-Tadema Sir Lawrence $2,800,000

Andre Carl $2,032,000

Archipenko Alexander $2,667,408

Arellano Juan $1,102,500

Arp Jean $2,800,000

Ast Balthasar van der $2,800,000

Avercamp Hendrick $8,688,000

Bacon Francis $27,598,245

Bakst Lev Samolovich $1,215,552

Balla Giacomo $4,400,000

Balthus Jean Balthasar Klossowski $6,736,000

Baraud Jean $1,200,000

Barcelo Miquel $1,574,683

Barocci Fredrico $2,600,000

Barry James $1,819,259

Bartolommeo Fra Baccio della Porta $9,750,000

Baselitz George $1,100,000

Basquiat Jean-Michel $5,509,500

Bazille Jean-Frederic $5,328,000

Beckman Max $22,560,000

Beert Osias $1,825,000

Beihong Xu $6,925,449

Bellotto Bernardo called II Canaletto Younger $5,642,000

Bellows George Wesley $27,502,500

Benson Frank Weston $1,821,000

Benton Thomas Hart $1,808,000

Beuckelaer Joachim $3,909,600

Bierstadt Albert $6,400,000

Blake William $3,928,000

Blakelock Ralph Albert $3,525,750

Bogdanov Belsky Nikolai Petrovich $1,360,000

Boldini Giovanni $1,500,000

Bomberg David $1,916,981

Bonnard Pierre $8,528,000

Bosschaert Ambrosius the Elder $2,400,000

Botero Fernando $2,032,000

Botticelli Sandro Alessandro
di Mariano Filepepi $16,000,000

Boucher Francois $2,166,000

Boudin Eugene $1,600,000

Bouguereau William Adolphe $3,526,000

Boulogne Jean called Valentin $1,200,000

Bourgeois Louise $10,700,000

Brack John $2,200,000

Brancusi Constantin $27,500,000

Braque George $8,640,000

Bravo Claudio $1,300,000

Bruce Patrick Henry $1,215,750

Brueghel the Elder Pieter $4,647,600

Brueghel Pieter II $9,555,555

Brueghel Jan $3,856,000

Brueghel Jan the Elder $1,687,440

Brush George de Forest $1,707,500

Bunker Dennis Miller $3,082,500

Buoninsegna Duccio di $45,000,000

Burne-Jones Edward $1,459,500

Burri Alberto $2,666,000

Caillebotte Gustave $14,300,000

Calder Alexander $4,185,750

Camarasa Hermenegildo Anglada $3,701,265

Canaletto Canale Giovanni Antonio $32,600,000

Cappelle Jan Van $6,242,900

Caravaggio aka Merisi Michelangelo $1,000,000

Carlevarijs Luca $2,000,000

Carracci Lodovico $13,703,703

Carracci Annibale $5,227,500

Cassatt Mary $4,072,500

Castiglione Giuseppe $2,291,500

Cattelan Maurizio $1,850,000

Ceruti Giacomo $1,642,012

Cezanne Paul $60,500,000

Chadwick Lynn $1,860,000

Chagall Marc $13,500,000

Chamberlain Jonh $1,024,000

Chardin Jean-Baptiste Simeon $2,400,000

Chase William Merritt $10,000,000

Chasseriau Theodore $1,029,840

Chillida Eduardo $3,748,148

Chun Liao Chi $2,462,724

Church Fredric Edwin $8,250,012

Cimabu $3,000,000

Claesz Pieter $1,000,000

Clausen Sir George $1,200,000

Close Chuck $3,208,000

Constable John $19,306,000

Copley John Singleton $1,696,000

Corot Jean-Baptiste Camille $2,811,000

Cotan Juan Sanchez $7,425,510

Courbet Gustave $8,460,000

Cranach Lucas the Elder $7,920,000

Credi Lorenzo di $1,805,000

Cropsey Jasper Francis $2,502,000

Cross Henri-Edmond $5,400,000

Cucchi Enzo $1,051,851

Cuypa Albert $5,852,000

Da Vinci Leonardo $31,800,000

Daddi Bernardo $2,400,000

Dali Salvador $4,126,680

Danqing Chen $1,472,000

Daqia Zhang Chang Dai Chien $2,307,600

Daumier Honore $2,248,800

David Jacques-Louis $6,250,000

Davis Stuart $2,422,500

De Kooning Elaine $1,142,500

De Kooning Willem $63,500,000

De Chirico Georgio $7,175,500

De Nittis Giuseppe $1,500,000

De Stael Nicolas $1,500,000

Degas Edgar $28,000,000

Del Sarto Andrea $11,395,000

Del Piombo Sebastiano $1,200,000

Delacroix Eugene $7,750,000

Delaunay Robert $5,170,000

Delvaux Paul $4,500,000

Derain Andre $6,848,000

Deutsch Ludwig $1,674,074

Dewing Maria Oakley $2,020,000

Diebenkorn Richard $6,176,000

Dix Otto $5,400,000

Doig Peter $1,547,169

Domenichino $3,000,000

Dominguez Oscar $1,149,367

Donatello $4,440,000

Dongen Kees van $9,200,000

Dossi Dosso $1,350,000

Dou Gerrit $2,042,620

Dreux Alfred de $1,400,000

Drost Willem $2,690,000

Drouais Francois Hubert $1,200,000

Drysdale Russell $1,017,250

Dubuffet Jean $5,000,000

Duchamp Marcel $1,762,500

Dufy Raoul $6,000,000

Dumas Marlene $6,300,000

Eakins Thomas C. $68,000,000

El Greco $5,775,000

Elsley Aurthur John $1,136,000

Ensor James $1,180,920

Ernst Max $2,429,500

Faberge Karl $9,600,000

Falk Robert Rafellovich $1,800,000

Fantin-Latour Henri $10,000,000

Farny Henry $1,212,500

Fautrier Jean $2,500,000

Feininger Lyonel $7,688,888

Figino Giovanni Ambrogio $1,400,000

Filonov Pavel Nikolaevich $1,760,992

Fischl Eric $1,920,000

Flanagan Barry $1,177,358

Fonatna Lucio $4,030,188

Foujita Tsuguharu $5,000,000

Fragonard Jean-Honore $8,000,000

Francis Sam Samuel Lewis $4,048,000

Francken Frans II $1,205,250

Freud Lucien $33,600,000

Friedrich Casper David $1,000,000

Frieseke Frederick C. $2,368,000

Friesz Emile-Othon $1,000,000

Gainsborough Thomas $7,000,000

Gaitonde Vasudev S $1,108,000

Galizia Fede $1,259,259

Gauguin Paul $40,330,000

Gentileschi Orazio $3,635,500

Gerard Francois $1,875,750

Gericault Theodore $5,249,210

Gerome Jean-Leon $3,083,120

Giacometti Alberto $103,900,000

Gifford Stanford $2,144,000

Giovanni de ser Giovanni di Simone $2,202,500

Glacken William James $1,550,000

Glover John $1,355,500

Goltzius Hendrick $1,500,000

Gontcharova Natalia $10,900,000

Gonzalez Julio $3,419,500

Gonzalez-Torres Felix $1,500,000

Gorky Arshile-V. $3,962,500

Gossaert Jan called Mabuse $1,652,500

Goya y Lucientes Francisco J. $7,020,000

Goyen Jan Van $1,875,765

Grigoriev Boris Dimitrievich $1,846,153

Gris Juan $8,479,500

Gros Baron Jean Antonie $2,346,775

Guanzhong Wu $1,194,960

Guardi Francesco $13,943,200

Guerard Eugene von $3,000,000

Guercino Giovanni Francesco Barbieri $2,367,350

Gursky Andreas $2,480,000

Guston Philip $1,835,500

Guy Francis $1,024,000

Hals Franz $12,350,000

Hals Dirk $1,047,500

Hamen Juan van der $1,158,997

Hammershoi Vilhelm $1,093,333

Harris Lawren $2,200,000

Hartley Marsden $1,652,500

Hassam Frederick Childe $20,000,000

Heade Martin Johnson $2,760,000

Heckel Erich $1,758,440

Heda William Claesz $1,430,000

Heem Jan Davidz de $6,000,000

Hepworth Barbara $2,600,000

Herring John Fredric $2,250,000

Hesse Eve $2,265,000

Hicks Edward $1,210,000

Hiepes Tomas $1,231,885

Hirst Damien $19,200,000

Hobbema Meindert $9,200,000

Hockney David $5,407,407

Hodler Ferdinand $2,125,850

Hoffmann Hans $2,645,000

Holbein Hans $2,400,000

Homer Winslow $36,000,000

Hooch Pieter de $2,000,000

Hopper Edward $26,800,000

Hulsdonck Jacob van $1,000,000

Hunt William Holman $1,000,000

Huysum, Jan Van

the younger $6,029,629

Indenbaum Leon $4,627,854

Ingres Jean-Auguste Dominique

$2,000,000

Jawlensky Alex von $8,296,000

Johns Jasper $80,000,000

Joli de Dipi Antonio $1,200,000

Jordaens Jacob $3,300,000

Jorn Asgar $2,099,500

Judd Donald $4,629,500

Kahlo Frida $5,616,000

Kandinsky Wassily $40,000,000

Kane Paul $3,300,000

Kapoor Anish $2,256,000

Kelly Mike $2,704,000

Kelly Ellsworth $2,600,000

Kensett John $1,248,000

Kessel Jan van $1,655,750

Kiefer Anselm $1,360,000

Kirchner Ernst Ludwig $38,100,000

Klee Paul $7,000,000

Klein Yves $4,720,000

Klimt Gustav $135,000,000

Kline Franz $6,400,000

Koekkoek Barend Cornelis $1,736,706

Kokoschka Oskar $2,700,000

Koons Jeff $25,800,000

Korovin Konstantin $1,696,000

Krasner Lee $3,170,000

Kustodiev Boris $2,900,000

Lam Wifredo $1,322,500

Lane Fritz Hugh $5,500,000

Laurencin Marie $1,300,000

Laurens Henri $1,472,000

Lavery John $1,983,240

Lawrence Sir Thomas $4,000,000

Le Sidaner Henri Eugene $1,360,000

Le Nain Louis $1,200,000

Le Brocquy Louis $1,750,000

Leger Fernand $22,407,500

Lehmbruck Wilhelm $1,212,500

Leighton Lord Frederick $1,923,680

Lempicka Tamara de Gorska

Lempitzki $8,500,000

Lewis John Frederick $1,150,000

Lichtenstein Roy $16,300,000

Liebermann Max $1,576,000

Lievens Jan $2,800,000

Liotard Jean-Etienne $1,800,000

Lipchitz Jaques $1,300,000

Lorenzetti Pietro $1,200,000

Lorrain Claude $2,095,750

Louis Morris $1,808,000

Lowry Laurence Stephen $3,000,000

Luttichuys Simon $1,528,888

Macke August $3,810,040

Magritte Rene $12,700,000

Maillol Aristide $2,800,000

Malevich Kasimir $17,000,000

Man Ray $1,504,440

Manet Edouard $24,000,000

Mantegna Andrea $28,600,000

Manzoni Piero $2,592,000

Maratta Carlo $1,100,000

Marc Franz $5,061,500

Marden Brice $1,875,750

Marieschi Michele $1,375,000

Marini Marino $2,687,680

Markovsky Konstantin $2,100,000

Marquet Albert $1,000,000

Martin Agnes $2,300,000

Mashkov Ilya $3,400,000

Matisse Henri $18,496,000

Matta Roberto $2,400,000

McCubbin Fredrick $1,778,750

Mehta Tyeb $1,584,000

Memling Hans $2,000,000

Menzel Adolf von $1,570,307

Merpes Adrian Jene $1,747,244

Messerschmidt Franz Xaver $1,800,000

Metcalf Willard Leroy $1,584,000

Michelangelo $11,400,000

Mignon Abraham $2,092,500

Millais John Everett $3,040,570

Millet Jean Francois $2,145,000

Miro Joan $12,600,000

Mitchell Joan $9,300,000

Modigliani Amedeo $31,300,000

Mola Pier Francisco $3,000,000

Mondrian Piet $40,000,000

Monet Claude $80,000,000

Moore Henry $6,167,500

Moran Thomas $2,752,500

Morandi Giorgio $1,300,000

Morbelli Angelo $2,202,500

Moreau Gustave $2,500,000

Morisot Berthe $3,850,000

Motherwell Robert $7,922,500

Munch Edvard $7,000,000

Munnings Sir Alfred James $7,848,000

Murillo Bartolome Esteban $4,230,770

Murkami Takashi $1,136,000

Nara Yoshitomo $1,080,000

Nauman Bruce $9,906,000

Newman Barnett $3,500,000

Nicholas of Munster Master $3,522,500

Nicholson Ben $2,115,000

Noguchi Isamu $1,248,000

Nolan Sidney $1,017,250

Noland Cady $6,600,000

Nolde Emil $1,500,000

Nussbaum Felix $1,758,440

O'Keeffe Georgia $6,166,000

Orpen Sir William $2,800,000

Ostade Adrian van $3,720,000

Oudry Jeane-Baptist $1,033,500

Pannini Giovanni Paolo $1,256,877

Parmigiano Girolano Fr. Mazzola $1,466,666

Parrish Fredric Maxfield $7,632,000

Peale Charles Wilson $21,296,000

Peale Rembrandt $3,000,000

Pechstein Max $1,400,740

Peeters Clars $1,684,000

Picabia Francis $4,780,880

Picasso Pablo $106,500,000

Pissarro Camille $14,601,000

Polke Sigmar $1,500,000

Pollock Jackson $140,000,000

Pontormo Jacopo Di Carruci il $35,200,000

Post Frans Jansz $4,512,500

Poussin Nicolas $21,050,000

Prendergast Maurice Brazil $3,256,000

Prince Richard $2,256,000

Raffaello Sanzio called Raphael $7,920,000

Ramos Martinez Alfredo $1,808,000

Ramos Mel $1,029,433

Ranney William T. $1,212,500

Rauschenberg Robert $7,260,000

Ray Charles $1,584,000

Redon Odilon $3,815,500

Redoute Pierre Joseph $1,300,000

Regnier Nicolas $1,543,650

Rembrandt Harmensz van Rijn $28,690,000

Remmington Fredric $5,172,500

Renoir Pierre Auguste $78,100,000

Repin Ilya $2,100,000

Reynolds Joshua $15,000,000

Ribera Jusepe de Spagnoletto $4,500,000

Ricco Andrea Briosco $4,740,300

Richter Gerhard $20,800,000

Rini Guido $2,816,000

Riopelle Jean Paul $1,600,000

Rivera Diego $3,082,500

Robert Hubert $6,237,037

Robinson Theodore $1,102,500

Rockwell Norman $15,400,000

Rodin Auguste $4,800,000

Roerich Nicholai Konstantinovich
Rerikh $2,200,000

Romano Giulio $2,406,700

Rothko Mark Marcus
Rothkowitz $3,000,000 $72,800,000

Rouault Georges $1,760,000

Rousseau Henri dit le
Douanier $4,047,980

Rubens Pieter Paul $76,600,000

Ruisdael Jacob van $4,752,620

Ruisdael Saloman van $1,105,750

Ruscha Ed $2,532,500

Rusinol Santiago $1,092,307

Russell Charles Marion $1,432,500

Ruzhou Cui $1,891,752

Ryman Robert $9,648,000

Rysselberghe Theo van $3,152,000

Saint Phalle Niki de $1,136,000

Salah Radel $1,900,000

Sanyu Chang Yu $3,758,354

Sargent John Singer $11,112,500

Savage Edward $1,102,500

Savery Roelandt $2,650,000

Schiele Egon $23,287,850

Schjerfbeck Helene Sofia $1,200,000

Schmidtt-Rottluff Karl $4,503,984

Schongauer Martin $1,779,000

Schreyvogel Charles $1,047,500

Scott William $1,113,962

Segantini Giovani $9,500,000

Serebriakova Zinaida Evegenievna $1,700,000

Serra Richard $4,500,000

Seurat Georges $35,200,000

Severini Gino $3,300,000

Shanren Bada $1,167,095

Shinn Everett $3,300,000

Shishkin Ivan $1,200,000

Siberecht Jan $1,100,000

Signac Paul $2,692,000

Signorin Telemaco $4,232,500

Silva Francis A $1,472,000

Sisley Alfred $3,000,000

Sloan John $2,205,750

Smith David $23,800,000

Somov Konstantin $5,184,615

Sorolla y Bastida Joaquin $3,173,000

Soulages Pierre $1,537,435

Soutine Chaim $9,449,856

Souza Francis Newton $1,360,000

Spencer Stanley $2,307,690

Spies Walter $1,130,000

Spitzweg Carl $1,072,320

Springer Cornelis $1,397,468

Stanley John Mix $1,652,000

Stella Frank $5,060,000

Stevens Alfred $1,625,000

Stewart Julius LeBlanc $2,312,000

Still Clyfford $61,000,000

Strindberg August Johan $4,057,450

Strong Brett-Livingstone $2,100,000

Stuart Gilbert $20,000,000

Stubbs George $4,700,000

Sweerts Michael $3,850,000

Tamayo Rufino $2,587,500

Tanguy Yves $2,250,000

Tansey Mark $3,040,000

Tayler Albert Chevallier $1,256,259

Teh-Chun Chu $3,364,400

Teniers David the Younger $5,700,000

Thiebaud Wayne $2,800,000

Tiepolo Giovanni Battista $2,202,500

Tingyan Zhang $7,000,000

Tissot James Jacques $5,282,500

Titian Tiziano Vecellio Di
Gregorio $13,555,000

Toulouse-Lautrec Henri de $22,416,000

Troy Francois de $3,600,000

Turner Joseph Mallord William $35,800,000

Tuttle Richard $1,054,000

Twombly Cy $7,968,000

Uklanski Piotr $1,071,698

Utrillo Maurice $1,454,180

Vallotton Felix $1,388,750

Van Dyck Anthony $3,100,000

Van Balen Hendrik $1,921,590

Van Gogh Vincent $82,500,000

Velasco Jose Maria $2,420,000

Velasquez Diego Rodriguez de Silva y $8,070,000

Velde Willem van de the Younger $2,800,000

Vereschagin Petr Pertovich $1,472,000

Vermeer Jan van der Meer
of Delft $30,000,000

Vernet Claud Joseph $1,540,000

Veronese Paolo Caliari $2,700,000

Verspronck Johannes Cornelisz $1,652,500

Villon Jacques $1,296,000

Vlaminck Maurice de $10,721,805

Vlieger Simon de $2,300,000

Vuillard Edouard $7,481,481

Waldmuller Ferdinand Georg $2,000,000

Walscapelle Jacob van $1,267,500

Wang Fu $1,500,000

Warhol Andy $71,700,000

Waterhouse John William $10,000,000

Watteau Jean-Antoine $3,185,600

Weeks Edwin Lord $1,570,500

Wesselman Thomas $2,656,603

Whistler James McNeil $2,866,000

Whiteley Brett $1,524,940

Whittredge Worthington $1,700,000

Wintenhalter Franz Xaver $1,961,760

Wittel Gaspar van $3,250,000

Wood Grant $6,960,000

Wool Christopher $1,696,000

Wou-Ki Zao $3,181,519

Wouwerman Philips $1,267,500

Wtewael Joachim Antonisz $5,000,000

Wyeth Andrew $7,000,000

Xiaogang Zhang $2,318,766

Yakolev Aleksandr Evgenevivh $1,900,000

Yeats Jack Butler $1,500,000

Yuskavage Lisa $1,024,000

Zampieri Domenico $3,302,000

Zoffany John $5,000,000

Zorn Anders $3,000,000

Zuniga Francesco $3,712,000

Zurbaran Francisco $2,095,000

Other periods of Art Styles with artists of that period

Courtesy of "The Art Signature File, by G. B. David" that also has many sales records and signatures

30,000 BC - 3000 BC [Prehistoric]

30,000 BC - 10,000 BC:Paleolithic

(Old Stone Age)

10,000 - 8000 BC: Mesolithic

(Middle Stone Age)

8000 - 3000 BC: Neolithic

(New Stone Age)

3000 BC - 331 BC [Ancient Civilizations]

3500 - 331 BC: Mesopotamian Art

3500 - 1750 BC: Sumerian/Akkadian

1000 - 539 BC:

Assyrian/Neo-Babylonian

539 - 331 BC: Persian

3200 - 1070 BC: Egyptian Art

3200 - 2185 BC: Old Kingdom

2040 - 1650 BC: Middle Kingdom

1550 - 1070 BC: New Kingdom

1370 - 1340 BC: Amarna Art

3000 - 1100 BC: Aegean Art

3000 - 1475 BC: Minoan (Crete)

1650 - 1100 BC: Mycenean (Greece)

1766 - 1045 BC: Shang Dynasty, China

1045 - 256 BC: Zhou Dynasty, China

800 BC - 337 AD [Classical Civilizations]

800 - 323 BC: Greek Art

323-150 BC: Hellenistic Art

6th - 5th century BC: Etruscan Art

509 BC - 337 AD: Roman Art

800 BC - 600 AD Olmec,Mexico

100 - 200 AD Zapotec, Mexico

2nd - 3rd c. AD Gandhara, India

373 - 1453 European Christian

Art/Middle Ages

200 - 732 Hiberno-Saxon &

400 - 1453 Byzantine Artist

Eulalios

Guido of Siena

Michael Astrapas and Eutychios

Theophanes the Cretan

Theophanes the Greek c. 1340 – c. 1410

Lazarus Zographos died 867

622 - 900 Islamic Art

732 - 900 Carolingian Art

900 - 1050 Ottonian Art

1000 - 1140 Romanesque Style

1140 - 1500 Gothic Style

320 - 647 Gupta, India

300 - 1500 Mayan, Mexico

618 - 907 Tang, China

645 - 791 Nara, Japan

960 - 1279 Song, China

1185 - 1333 Kamakura, Japan

1350 - 1520 Aztec, Mexico

1100 - 1532 Inca, Peru

1299 - 1923 Ottoman, Turkish Artists

Halil Pasa (1857-1939)

Zekai Pasa (1860-1919)

Hoca Ali Riza (1864-1939)

Osman Asaf (1868-1938)

Ahmet Ziya (1869-1938)

Sevket Dag (1876-1944) $3000

Sami Yetik (1878-1945)

Nazmi Ziya (1881-1937)

Hikmet Onat (1882-1977)

Ibrahim Calli (1882-1960) $125,000

Huseyin Hasim (-1930)

Avni Lifij (1886-1927

Feyhaman Duran (1886-1970)

Mufide Kadri (1890-1912)

Osman Hamdi Bey (1842-1910) $700,000

Abdulcelil Levni or Abdulcelil

Çelebi (- 1732)

Seker Ahmed Pasha (1841–1907)

Hâfiz Osman (1642 – 1698)

Sheikh Hamdullah (1436–1520)

Mid 19th to 20th Century Artists

Osman Hamdi Bey (1842-1910)

$700,000

Seker Ahmet Pasha (1841-1907)

Sayyid Suleyman (1842-1913)

Halil Pasha (1860-1939)

Zekai Pasha (1860-1919)

Hodja Ali Riza (1858-1930)

Ahmet Ziya Akbulut (1869-1938)

(1914 Generation) Artists

Nazmi Ziya Guran (1881–1937)

Ms. Mihri Merciful

Adil Omar

Fixed Feyhaman

Huseyin Avni Lifij

Ibrahim Calli $125,000

Mehmet Ruhi Arel

Müstakiller (The Independents) Artists

Turgut Zaim (1906-1974)

R. Fazil (Epikman) (1902-1974)

Cevat Hamit (Dereli) (1900-1989)

Seref Kamil (Akdik) (1862-1941)

Mahmut Fehmi (Cuda) (1904-1987)

Nurullah Cemal (Berk) (1906-1981)

Hale Asaf (1905-1938)

Ali Avni (Çelebi) (1904-1993)

Ahmet Zeki (Kocamemi) (1900-1959)

Muhittin Sebati (1901-1935)

Ratip Asir (Acudoglu) (1898-1957)

Fahrettin Arkunlar (1901-1971)

Ilhan Demirci

Sefik Bursali

Semsi Arel

Maide Arel

Abidin Elderoglu

Hamit Görele

Ziya Keseroglu

Seyfi Toray

Fikret Mualla

Cemal Bingöl

Nejat Devrim

Eren EyubogluFüreyya Kiliç

Adnan Coker

Lütfü Günay

Selim Turan (1915-1994)

Fahrunissa Zeid (1901-1991)

Adnan Turani (1925-)

Detached "D Group" Artists

Turgut Zaim (1906-1974)

R. Fazil (Epikman) (1902-1974)

Cevat Hamid (Dereli) (1900-1989)

Honor Akdik (1862-1941)

Mahmut Cuda (1904-1987)

Bensu Girgin (1905-1938)

Ali Avni (Chalabi) (1904-1993)

Intelligent Kocamemi (1900-1959)

Muhittin Sebati (1901-1935)

Ratip Asir (Acudoglu)

(1898-1957), sculptor

Fahrettin Arkunlar

(1901-1971) decorator

Alsan Alfred Mar (Marengo)

(1914-1981), painter

Zeki Faik Izer (1905-1988)

Nurullah Berk (1906-1981)

Elif Naci (1898-1988)

Cemal Tollu (1899-1968)

Abidin Dino (1913-1993)

Zuhtu Muridoglu (1906-1992)

Bedri Rahmi Eyuboglu (1911-1975)

Eren Eyuboglu (1913-1988)

Halil Dikmen (1906-1964)

Esref Üren (1897-1984)

Sabri Berkel (1907-1993)

Hakki Anli (1906-1990)

Arif Kaptan (1906-1979)

Salih Uralli (1908-1984)

"E Group" artists

Zeki Faik Izer (1905-1988)

Nurullah Berk (1906-1981)

Elif Naci (1898-1988)

Jamal Tollu (1899-1968)

Abidin Dino (1913-1993)

Zühtü Müridoglu (1906-1992) sculptor

Bedri Rahmi Eyuboglu (1911-1975)

Eren Eyuboglu (1913-1988)

Halil Dikmen (1906-1964)

Ashraf Üren (1897-1984)

Sabri Berkel (1907-1993)

Anli Rights (1906-1990)

Captain Arif (1906-1979)

Salih Uralli (1908-1984)

Ilhan Blacksmith

Bursa Sefik

Leyla Gamsiz

Shams-Arel

Maide Arel

Abidin Elderoglu

Hamid Görele

Zia Keseroilu

Toray Seyfi

Cemal Bingol

Nejat Revolution

Eren Eyuboglu

Sword Füreyya

Adnan Coker

Lutfi Gunay

Selim Turan (1915-1994)

Hasan Kavruk (1918-2007)

Fahrunissa Zeid (1901-1991)

Adnan Turanian (1925 -)

"Yeniler Grubu"
(The Newcomers Group) late 1930s

"New Group" Artists

Iyem Nuri (1915-2005)

Turgut Atalay

Avni Arbas (1919-2003)

Selim Turan

Ferruh Basaga

Eda Stops

Kemal Sönmezler

Mumtaz Manson

Agop Arad

Akal Hasmet

Oktay Günday

The Conquest King (1916-1977)

Nuri Iyem (1915-2005)

Mümtaz Yener

Turgut Zaim

Cihat Burak

"Onlar Grubu" (The Group Ten)
"Tens Group" (1947) Artists

Mustafa Esirku

Turan Erol

Rebecca Otyam

When they arrive, Adnan

Leyla Gamsiz

Hulusi Sarpturk

Nedim Gunsur

Fikret Otyam

Orhan Peker

Mehmet Pesen

Adnan Varinca

"Yeni Dal Grubu" (The New Branch Group)
"New Major Group" (1959) Artists
A current focus on social reality.

Ibrahim Balaban

Avni Mehmetoglu

Ihsan Incesu

Kemal Incesu

Sahin FUNDA

Rights Torunoglu

Siyah Kalem Grubu

(The Black Pen Group) 1961 Artists

Cemal Bingöl

Ismail Altinok

Selma Arel

Lütfü Günay

Ihsan Cemal Karaburcak

Asuman Kiliç

Ayse Silay

Solmaz Tugac

Other notable Turkish Artists

Ear Husamettin

Ahmet Saral

A. Aydin Baykara

Peters Varol

Ercument Kalmek

Joy Erdok

Ahmet Günestekin

Ercan Süelden

Rahmi Pehlivanli

Neriman Oyman

Murat Külcüoglu

Semih Know

Cetin Scholar

Melih Ozturk

Oktay Anilamert

Ekrem Kahraman

Alpine Temur Ulukiliç

Gunay Demir

Tuncer Sabahattin

Loyal and Nilufer Isbilen

Mustafa Ucbilek

Fikret Mualla

Friday Furnace

Fevzi Karakoç

Habib Aydogdu

Ismail Hunter

View Kapçak

Suleyman Saim Tekcan

Orhan Umut

Nilgun Irmikçi

Yusuf Demirtas

Demirtas Muhteber

Ahmet Atan

Ramiz Aydin

Noble, Rasim

Rock Tanyeri

Salih Cengiz

Gurhan Yucel

Ayhan Taskiran

Sadat Kumova

Selahattin Aydi

Iranian Artists Ancient Persia

Mani

Muhammad ibn Zakariya al-Razi

Classical Islamic Persia

Kamaleddin Behzad

Reza Abbasi

Farrukh Beg

Mihr 'Ali

Modern era

Aghdashloo, Aydin

Alamir, Alaleh

Alivandi, Bahram

Arabshahi, Massoud (1935-)

Aram, Kamrooz (1978-)

Siah Armajani

Behzad, Hossein

Ali Divandari

Delara Darabi

Iran Darroudi

Abolhassan Etessami (1903–1978)

Fakhr Yaseri, Farzin

Ghanbari, Mokarrameh (1928–2005)

Ghandriz, Mansoor

Marcos Grigorian

Khosrow Hassanzadeh

Haydar Hatemi

Mansooreh Hosseini

Mehdi Hosseini

Kamal-ol-Molk

Kazemi, Zhaleh (1944–2005)

Shokoufeh Kavani

Farideh Lashai (1944-)

Tannaz Lahiji (1978-)

Iman Maleki

Farshid Mesghali (1943-)

Mohsen Vaziri-Moghaddam (1924-)

Farhad Moshiri

Noreen Motamed

Mir-Hossein Mousavi (1941-)

Neshat, Shirin

Nouri, Mina (1951-)

Novin, Guity (1944-)

Kazem Ordoobadi (1919–2002)

Rassouli, Freydoon

Sadeghi, Ali Akbar (1937-)

Sadr, Behjat

Salimi, Homayoun (1948-)

Samad, Khwaja Abdus (16th century)

Sohrab Sepehri

Shokof, Daryush

Shafrazi, Tony

Sadeghi Amini, Farhad

Towhidi Tabari (1964-)

Jazeh Tabatabai (1931–2008)

Mohammad Ali Taraghijah

Parviz Tanavoli

Mohsen Vaziri-Moghaddam

Zenderoudi, Hossein (1937-)

Ziapour, Jalil

Chinese Artists

1368 - 1644 Ming, China

Dai Jin

Wu Wei

Lan Ying

Lin Liang

Tang Yin

Wen Zhengming

Shenzhou

Qiu Ying

Xu Wei

Chen chun

Zhao Zuo

Dong Qichang

Japanese Ming Artist

Sesshu Toyo

1392 - 1573 Muromachi, Japan Artists

Sesshu Toyo

Mokkei (circa 1250)

Mokuan Reien (d.1345)

Kao Ninga (e.14th century)

Mincho (1352-1431)

Josetsu (1405-1423)

Tenshe Shebun(d.1460)

Sesshe Teye (1420-1506)

Kano Masanobu (1434-1530)

Kano Motonobu (1476-1559)

1573 - 1603 Azuchi-Momoyama period, Japan Artists

Kano Eitoku (1543-1590)

Kano Sanraku (1559-1663)

Kano Tanyu (1602-1674)

Hasegawa Tohaku (1539-1610)

Kaiho Yusho (1533-1615)

1550 - 1680 Benin, Africa
1615 - 1868 Edo, Japan Artists

Tawaraya Statsu (d.1643)

Ogata Korin (1658-1716)

Gion Nankai (1677-1751)

Sakaki Hyakusen (1697-1752)

Yanagisawa Kien (1704-1758)

Yosa Buson (1716-1783)

Ito Jakuchu (1716-1800)

Ike no Taiga (1723-1776)

Maruyama Okyo (1733-1795)

Okada Beisanjin (1744-1820)

Uragami Gyokudo (1745-1820)

Matsumura Goshun (1752-1811)

Katsushika Hokusai (1760-1849)

Tani Buncho (1763-1840)

Tanomura Chikuden (1777-1835)

Okada Hanko (1782-1846)

Yamamoto Baiitsu (1783-1856)

Watanabe Kazan (1793-1841)

Utagawa Hiroshige (1797-1858) $100,000

Shibata Zeshin (1807-1891)

Tomioka Tessai (1836-1924)

1868 - 1945 Prewar period Japan Artists

Harada Naojiro (1863-1899)

Yamamoto Hosui (1850-1906)

Asai Chu (1856-1907)

Kano Hogai (1828-1888)

Hashimoto Gaho (1835-1908)

Kuroda Seiki (1866-1924)

Wada Eisaku (1874-1959)

Okada Saburosuke (1869-1939)

Sakamoto Hanjiro (1882-1962)

Aoki Shigeru (1882-1911)

Fujishima Takeji (1867-1943)

Yokoyama Taikan 1868-1958

Hishida Shunso 1874-1911

Kawai Gyokudo 1873-1957

Uemura Shoen (1875-1949)

Maeda Seison 1885-1977

Shimomura Kanzan 1873-1930

Takeuchi Seiho 1864-1942

Tomioka Tessai 1837-1924

Uemura Shoen 1875-1949

Shimomura Kanzan (1873-1930)

Hishida Shunso (1874-1911)

Imamura Shiro (1880-1916)

Tomita Keisen (1879-1936)

Koide Narashige (1887-1931)

Kishida Ryusei (1891-1929)

Yorozu Tetsugoro (1885-1927)

Hayami Gyoshu (1894-1935)

Kawabata Ryushi (1885-1966)

Tsuchida Hakusen (1887-1936)

Murakami Kagaku (1888-1939)

Yasui Sotaro (1881-1955)

Sanzo Wada (1883-1967)

Umehara Ryuzaburo (1888-1986)

Yasuda Yukihiko (1884-1978)

Kobayashi Kokei (1883-1957)

Leonard Foujita (1886-1968)

Yuzo Saeki (1898-1928)

Ito Shinsui 1898-1972

Kaburaki Kiyokata 1878-1972

Takehisa Yumeji 1884-1934

1945 - present Postwar period Japan Artists

Ogura Yuki (1895-2000)

Uemura Shoko 1902-2001

Koiso Ryouhei (1903-1988)

Kaii Higashiyama (1908-1999)

Japanese Woodblock artists

Hishikawa Moronobu (1618-1694)

Torii Kiyonobu I (c.1664-1729)

Suzuki Harunobu (1724-1770)

Torii Kiyonaga (1752-1817)

Utamaro (ca. 1753-1806)

Sharaku (active 1794-1795)

Hokusai (1760-1849)

Toyokuni (1769-1825) $156,500

Keisai Eisen (1790-1848)

Kunisada (1786-1865)

Hiroshige (1797-1858) $100,000

Kuniyoshi (1797-1861)

Kunichika (1835-1900)

Chikanobu (1838-1912)

Yoshitoshi (1839-1892)

Ogata Gekko (1859-1920)

1644 - 1912 Qing, China Artists

Gong Xian (ca. 1618-1689)

Fan Qi (1615/1616-ca. 1694)

Ye Xin (fl. 1650-1670s)

Zou Zhe (1636-ca. 1708)

Gao Cen (fl. 1670s; d. 1689)

Hu Zao (fl. 1681)

Wu Hong (fl. 1670s-1680s)

Xie Sun (fl. 1679)

Ju Chao Chü Ch'ao (1811-1865)

Chen Hongshou Ch'en

Hung-shou (1598-1652)

Dai Xi Tai Hsi (1801-1860)

Wang ShìShèn (1686-1759)

Huáng Shèn (1687-1768)

Li Shàn (1686-1756)

Jin Nóng (1687-1764)

Luo Pìn (1733-1799)

Gao Xiáng (1688-1753)

Zhèng Xiè Zhèng BanQiáo (1693-1765)

Li FangYing (1696 - 1755)

Fei Danxu Fei Tan-hsü 1801-1850

Gai Qi 1774-1829

Gong Xian (ca. 1618-1689)

Fan Qi (1615/1616-ca. 1694)

Ye Xin (fl. 1650-1670s)

Zou Zhe (1636-ca. 1708)

Gao Cen (fl. 1670s; d. 1689)

Hu Zao (fl. 1681)

Wu Hong (fl. 1670s-1680s)

Xie Sun (fl. 1679)

Gao Fènghàn (1683–1749)

Gao Qípeì (1660-1734)

Gao Xiang (1688–1753)

Gong Xian

Kung Hsien) (1618–1689

Gu Yun Ku Yün, 1835—1896)

Ding Guanpeng Ting

Kuan-p'eng) (active 1708-1771)

Hong Ren Hongren 1610-1663

Hu Zaobin

Wu Cho Bun 1897-1942)

Hua Yan Hua Yen; 1682 – 1756)

Huáng Binhóng (1865-1955

Huang Shen (1687 – 1772

Jiang Tingxi Chiang

T'ing-hsi, 1669–1732

Jiao Bengzhen Chiao

Ping-chen 1689–1726

Jin Nong 1687-1764

Jin Tingbiao

Ju Lian Chü Lien; 1828-1904

Kun Cán 1612 – 1674

Lam Qua Kwan Kiu

Cheong Lam Kwan; 1801–1860

Leng Mei 1677-1742

Li Fangying (1696–1755)

Li Shan 1686–1756)

Luo Mu (1622–1706)

Luo Ping Lo P'ing 1733 - 1799)

Min Zhen 1730 -)

Ni Tian 1855–1919)

Qi Baishi 1864 - 1957

Rèn Yí 1840-1896)

Ren Xiong 1823-1857

Bada Shanren

Pata Shanjen Zhu Da

Pat-thai San-nin, 1626—1705)

Shen Nanpin or Shen Nan-p'in,

Shen Ch'uan 1682 - c. 1780

Zha Shibiao 1615-1698

Shih T'ao Zhu Ruoji (1642–1718

Bian Shoumin 1684–1752

Yun Shouping

Wu Li

Wang Shimin (1592-1680)

Wang Jian (1598-1677)

Wang Hui (1632-1717)

Wang Yuanqi (1642-1715)

Wáng Hui; 1632–1717

Wang Shishen (1686–1759)

Wang Chen Wang Zhen 1867–1938

Wu Chang-shih

(Wu Changshou) (1843–1927)

Wú Changshuò 1844-1927

Xu Beihong 1895-1953

Yang Borun Yang Peifu

Yang Pojun, 1837–1911

I Fukyu Yi Hai 1700's

Pan Yuliang,

born Zhang Yuliang (1899–1977

Yun Shouping Nantian (1633–1690

Zhang Yin 1761-1829)

Zhang Zongcang 1686–1756)

Zhao Zhiqian 1829-1884)

Zhèng Xiè Zheng Banqiao (1693–1765)

Zhou Shuxi Chou Shu-hsi 1624–1705)

Zou Yigui Tsou I-kui

Yuanbao (1686–1772),

1400 - 1600 Renaissance Artists

Artists of the Italian Renaissance
Bellini

Botticelli

Cimabue

Crivelli

Donatello

Fra Angelico

Fra Carnevale

Ghiberti

Ghirlandaio

Giorgione

Giotto

Leonardo da Vinci

Fra Lippi

Lotto

Mantegna

Martini

Masaccio

Michelangelo $11,400,000

Piero della Francesca

Piero di Cosimo

Raphael

Tintoretto

Titian

Uccello

Veronese

Northern Renaissance

Altdorfer

Bosch

Bruegel

Cranach

Gerard David

Dürer

van der Goes

Grünewald

Holbein

Memling

van Eyck

van der Weyden

1600 - 1700 Baroque Artists

Caravaggio $1,000,000

Peter Paul Rubens $76,600,000

Rembrandt van Rijn $28,690,000

Frans Hals $12,350,000

Anthony Van Dyck $3,100,000

Gianlorenzo Bernini

Jacob Jordaens

Louis Le Nain

1600 - 1700 Rococo Period Artists

Francesco Guardi $13,943,200

Francois Boucher $2,166,000

Jean Honore Fragonard $8,000,000

Thomas Gainsborough $7,000,000

Rosalba Carriera

Francois Desportes

Jean Baptiste Chardin $2,400,000

1700 - 1750 Rococo Artists

Jean-Antoine Watteau (1684-1721) $3,185,600

François Boucher (1703-1770)

Jean-Honoré Fragonard (1732-1806) $8,000,000

Thomas Gainsborough's (1727-1788) $7,000,000

Élisabeth-Louise Vigée-Le Brun's (1755-1842)

Jean François de Troy (1679-1752)

Jean-Baptiste van Loo (1685-1745

Louis-Michel van Loo (1707-1771)

Charles-Amédée-Philippe van Loo (1719-1795)

Charles-André van Loo (1705-1765)

Nicolas Lancret (1690-1743)

Jean-Baptiste-Siméon Chardin(1699-1779) $2,400,000

Jean-Baptiste Greuze (1725-1805)

William Hogarth (1697-1764)

Francis Hayman (1708-1776)

Angelica Kauffman (1741-1807)

Thomas Gainsborough (1727-1788) $7,000,000

Joshua Reynolds (1723-1792) $15,000,000

Antony Van Dyck (1599-1641) $3,100,000

Maurice Quentin de La Tour (1704-1788)

1800 - 1880 Pre-Modern Artists

Beardsley, Aubrey (1872-1898) $49,000

Bonnard, Pierre (1867-1947) $8,528,000

Braque, Georges (1882-1963) $8,640,000

Caillebotte, Gustave (1848-1894) $14,300,000

Cassatt, Mary (1845-1926) $4,072,500

Cezanne, Paul (1839-1906)$60,500,000

Chagall, Marc (1887-1985) $13,500,000

Courbet, Gustave (1819-1877) $8,460,000

Dali, Salvador (1904-1989) $4,126,680

Daumier, Honore (1808-1879) $2,248,800

Dufy, Raoul (1877-1953) $6,000,000

Eakins, Thomas (1844-1916) $68,000,000

Ernst, Max (1891-1976) $2,429,500

Gauguin, Paul (1848-1903)$40,330,000

Gogh, Vincent Van (1853-1890) $82,500,000

Hassam, Childe (1859-1935) $20,000,000

Homer, Winslow (1836-1910) $36,000,000

Itten, Johannes (1888-1967) $25,000

Kokoschka, Oskar (1886-1980) $2,700,000

Lichenstein, Roy (b.1923)

Manet, Edouard (1832-1883) $24,000,000

Matisse, Henri (1869-1954) $18,496,000

Meissonier, Ernest (1815-1890)

Miro, Joan (1893-1983) $12,600,000

Modigliani, Amedeo (1884-1920) $31,300,000

Mondrian, Piet (1872-1944) $40,000,000

Monet, Claude (1840-1944) $80,000,000

Motherwell, Robert (b.1915)$7,922,500

Mucha, Alphonse (1860-1939) $100,000

Munch, Edvard (1863-1944) $7,000,000

Picasso, Pablo Ruiz y (1881-1973) $106,500,000

Pisarro, Camille (1831-1903) $14,601,00

Poussin, Nicholas (1593-1665) $21,050,000

Ray, Man (1890-1976) $1,504,440

Renoir, Pierre Auguste $78,100,000

Roualt, Georges (1871-1958) $1,760,000

Seurat, Georges (1859-1891) $35,200,000

Toulouse- Lautrec, Henri

Marie Raymond de (1864-1901) $22,416,000

Valadon, Suzanne (1867-1938)

1750 –1880 Neo-Classicism Artists

Jean-Baptiste-Simeon Chardin $2,400,000

Nicolas Poussin $21,050,000

Jacques-Louis David $6,250,000

Jean-Auguste-Dominique

Ingres $2,000,000

1800 - 1880 Romanticism Artists

Caspar David Friedrich $1,000,000

Henry Fuseli

Eugene Delacroix

Theodore Gericault $5,249,210

1830's - 1870 Realism Artists

Luitpold Adam

Alexandre Antigna

Fedor Antonov

Octav Boncile

Lyndall Bass

Adolf von Becker

Marcus Beilby

Kent Bellows

Bikash Bhattacharjee

Julien Le Blant

Rosa Bonheur $491,000

François Bonvin

Columbano Bordalo Pinheiro

William-Adolphe Bouguereau $3,526,000

Hippolyte Boulenger

Robert Brackman

Jules Breton $1,250,000

Fidelia Bridges

Harold Bruder

Derek Buckner

Ernesto de la Cárcova

Albert Charpin

Edward Leigh Chase

Frank Swift Chase

Manon Cleary

Mikhail Konstantinovich Clodt

Jack Coggins

William Coldstream

Paul Collins

Alex Colville

Gustave Courbet $8,460,000

Josef Dande

Charles-François Daubigny

Rackstraw Downes

Dragan Malesevic Tapi

Joseph Ducreux

Julien Dupré

Thomas Eakins $68,000,000

John Englehart

Giovanni Fattori

Neil Faulkner

Károly Ferenczy

Émile Friant

Nikolai Ge

Evan Goldman

Gavriil Gorelov

Antonio Guzmán Capel

Mauritz de Haas

Harijadi Sumodidjojo

Ralph Hedley

Heinrich Mücke

John Frederick Herring, Sr. $2,250,000

Jacques Hnizdovsky

Simon Hollósy

Winslow Homer $36,000,000

Conrad Hommel

Clark Hulings

Valery Jacobi

Mathurin Janssaud

Eero Järnefelt

Paja Jovanovic

Kitty Lange Kielland

Ruslan Korostenskij

Simon Kozhin

Ivan Kramskoi

Arkhip Kuindzhi

Henry Herbert La Thangue

Wilhelm Leibl

Dana Levin

Isaac Levitan

Nestor Leynes

Antonio López García

Aleksandr Makovsky

Édouard Manet $24,000,000

Ans Markus

Theodor Martens

Stan Masters

Anton Mauve

Vassily Maximov

Paul Meltsner

Edward Middleditch

Jean-François Millet

Apollon Mokritsky

Archibald Herman Muller

Grigoriy Myasoyedov

Stephen Namara

Volodymyr Orlovsky

Alexander Osmerkin

Otto Erdmann

Vasily Perov

Paul Philippoteaux

Arkady Plastov

Vasily Polenov

James Pollard

Uroš Predi

Paul Alexandre Protais

Illarion Pryanishnikov

Josip Rai

Ilya Repin

Théodule Ribot

Manuel Lopes Rodrigues

Théodore Rousseau

Konstantin Savitsky

Alexei Savrasov

August Schneider

Valentin Serov

Ivan Shishkin

Alan Shuptrine

Dmitri Sinodi-Popov

Isaac Soyer

Raphael Soyer

R. B. Sprague

Johann Gottfried Steffan

Vasily Surikov

Henry Jones Thaddeus

Mór Than

Alton Tobey

William B. T. Trego

Konstiantyn Trutovsky

Fyodor Vasilyev

Viktor Vasnetsov

Vasily Vereshchagin

Nicolae Vermont

Antoine Vollon

Pedro Weingärtner

Harold Weston

Geoff Williams

Nicholas Charles Williams

Nikolai Yaroshenko

Félix Ziem

1848 –1854 Pre-Raphaelites Artists

Ford Madox Brown

Edward Burne-Jones

William Holman Hunt

John Everett Millais

Dante Gabriel Rossetti

1870's - 1890's Impressionism Artists

Jean-Baptiste-Camille Corot $2,811,000

Gustave Courbet $8,460,000

Charles-François Daubigny

Edouard Manet $24,000,000

Theodore Rousseau

Frederic Bazille

Eugene Boudin $1,600,000

Gustave Caillebotte $14,300,000

Mary Cassatt $4,072,500

Paul Cézanne

Edgar Degas $28,000,000

Claude Monet $80,000,000

Berthe Morisot $3,850,000

Camille Pissarro $14,601,000

Pierre-Auguste Renoir $78,100,000

Alfred Sisley $3,000,000

Paul Gauguin $40,330,000

Childe Hassam $20,000,000

Georges Seurat $35,200,000

Hudson River School Artists

Albert Bierstadt

Frederick Church

Thomas Cole

Asher B. Durand

Martin Johnson Heade

George Inness

John F. Kensett $1,200,000

Thomas Moran

1870 - 1910 Symbolism Artists

William Blake

Henry Fuseli

Gustave Moreau

Puvis de Chavannes

Odilon Redon

Gustav Klimt $135,000,000

Aubrey Beardsley $49,000

Edvard Munch $7,000,000

Arnold Boecklin

Leon Spilliaert

1890's Nabis Artists

Paul Sérusier and Maurice Denis were the main artists of the group. Other group artists were Édouard Vuillard, Pierre Bonnard, Aristide Maillol, and Félix Vallotton. The group held its first exhibition in 1892. Nabis was greatly influenced by the artist Paul Gauguin,

1880 - 1945 Modernism

Mary Abbott

Julio Abril

Philip Absolon

Jorge Figueroa Acosta

Valerio Adami

Nadir Afonso

Nadir Afonso artworks

Yaacov Agam

Roger Aguilar Labrada

Julio Aguilera

Raúl Alfaro Torres

Else Alfelt

Joe Allen

Charles Alston

Jean-Michel Atlan

Nathan Altman

Pedro Álvarez Castelló

Roberto Álvarez Ríos

Tarsila do Amaral

Michael Peter Ancher

Caesar Andrade Faini

Constantine Andreou

Rita Angus

Anelia Pavlova (Annael)

Timothy App

Karel Appel

Dominique Appia

Alexis Arapoff

Félix Arauz

Yolande Ardissone

Armando de Armas Romero

Salma Arastu

Stylianos Atteshlis

Frank Auerbach

Edward Avedisian

Milton Avery

Esteban Ayala Ferrer

Manuel Azadigian

Philip Aziz

Francis Bacon $27,598,000

Georges Badin

Blažej Baláž

Mária Balážová

Juan Ballester Carmenates

John Balossi

Balthus

Will Barnet

Rex Barrat

Georg Baselitz

Rudolf Bauer

Wolfgang Bauer

A. S. Baylinson

William Baziotes $300,000

John Beard

Romare Bearden

Timothy Behrens

Hilda Belcher

Hans Bellmer

George Bellows $27,502,500

Federico Beltrán Masses

Mario Bencomo

Anthony Benjamin

Martin Benka

Thomas Hart Benton $1,808,000

Aaron Berkman

Abraham Berline

Cundo Bermúdez

José Bernal

André Beronneau

Norma Bessouet

Robert Bevan

Remo Bianco

Edward Biberman

Sebastian Bieniek

Ejler Bille

Elmer Bischoff

Piran Bishop

Louis Bissinger

Emil Bisttram

Carl Blair

Ralph Albert Blakelock

Norman Blamey

Arnold Blanch

Fritz Bleyl

Godfrey Blow

Oscar Florianus Bluemner

Abraham Bogdanove

Alexander Bogomazov

Maurice Boitel

Gina Bold

Claude Bonin-Pissarro

Pierre Bonnard $8,528,000

Emery Bopp

Paul-Émile Borduas

Fernando Botero

Stanley Boxer

Juan Boza Sánchez

Christopher Bramham

Peter Brandes

Maurice Braun

Rudolf Bredow

Julio Breff

George Hendrik Breitner

Jean Brenner

James E. Brewton

Ernest Briggs

María Brito

Josephine Broekhuizen

Franz Bronstert

Bertram Brooker

Angie Elizabeth Brooksby

Judith Brown

Theophilus Brown

Patrick Henry Bruce $1,215,750

Albín Brunovský

Jean Paul Brusset

Carl Buchheister

Erich Buchholz

Adriano Buergo

Charles Ragland Bunnell

Barry Burman

Jack Bush

Arturo García Bustos

Francis Cadell

Paul Cadmus

Lawrence Calcagno

Sergio de Camargo

Steven Campbell

Heinrich Campendonk

Arthur Beecher Carles

Renée Carpentier-Wintz

Oreste Carpi

Matthew Carr

Mario Carreño Morales

Carter

Felice Casorati

Henry Casselli

Bertrand Castelli

Clément Castelli

Carlos Catasse

Giorgio Cavallon

Miguel Cerejido

Ferro Milone Cesare

Marc Chagall $13,500,000

Nora Chapa Mendoza

Elizabeth Charleston

Émilie Charmy

Doris Totten Chase

Edward Leigh Chase

Frank Swift Chase

Junko Chodos

Dan Christensen

Jean Camille Cipra

Geneviève Claisse

Margaret Clarkson

James Clifford

Edmund Thomas Clint

Carroll Cloar

Charles Cobelle

Juan Fernando Cobo

Robert Colescott

Nusret Çolpan

Robert Colquhoun

Alex Colville

Miguel Condé

John Connell

Daniel Conrad

Theo Constanté

Alfred L. Copley

Thomas Cornell

Rafael Coronel

Xavier Cortada

Shane Cotton

Jonathon Coudrille

Rosemary Cove

Jan Cox

Jack Crabtree

Tullio Crali

Susanne Crane

Ralston Crawford

Joseph Crawhall III

Dennis Creffield

Odile Crick

Charles Crodel

Jean Crotti

Miguel Cubiles

Liliam Cuenca

Greg Curnoe

George Cuthbertson

Oscar D'Amico

Salvador Dalí

Adelaide Damoah

Allan D'Arcangelo

Nils von Dardel

Andrew Dasburg

Fernand Dauchot

Thomas Nathaniel Davies

Gene Davis

Ronald Davis

Stuart Davis $2,422,500

Heinrich Maria Davringhausen

David Dawson

Francis de Erdely

Nanno de Groot

Eugène de Kermadec

Willem de Kooning $63,500,000

Niki de Saint Phalle $1,136,000

Nicolas de Stael $1,500,000

Alicia DeBrincat

Sonia Delaunay $3,900,000

Charles Demuth

André Derain $6,848,000

Philippe Derome

Preston Dickinson

Richard Diebenkorn $6,176,000

Burgoyne Diller $100,000

Jim Dine $250,000

Abidin Dino

Jessica Dismorr

Otto Dix $5,400,000

Jasmina Djokic

Theo van Doesburg $200,000

Vicente Dolpico Lerner

Jan Domela

Enrico Donati

Jelena Dorotka

John Dos Passos

Katherine Sophie Dreier

Elsie Driggs

Albert Dubois-Pillet

Jean Dubuffet $5,000,000

Raoul Dufy $6,000,000

Edward Dugmore

Daniel du Janerand

Lucien Dulfan

Bernard Dumaine

Roy Turner Durrant

Friedel Dzubas

Ellen Eagle

Alan Ebnother

Eero Nelimarkka

Louis Eilshemius

Aleksandra Ekster

Daniel Enkaoua

Ramon Enrich

Arthur John Ensor

Max Ernst $2,429,500

Otgonbayar Ershuu

Miguel de la Espriella

Stephen Etnier

Nicholas Evans

Paterson Ewen

Julius Exter

Demetrios Farmakopoulos

Gary Farrelly

Yankel Feather

Mary Fedden

Paul Feeley

Lyonel Feininger $7,688,888

Manuel Felguérez

John Duncan Fergusson

Joshua Field

Emil Filla

John Shelton

Perle Fine

Tony Fomison

Eric Forbes-Robertson

Noel Forster

Graham Forsythe

Tsuguharu Foujita $1,265,000

Sam Francis $4,048,000

Siron Franco

Jane Frank

Mary Frank

Wilhelm Freddie

Mark Freeman

Lima de Freitas

Suzy Frelinghuysen

Jared French

Lucian Freud $33,600,000

Otto Freundlich

Arnold Friberg

Pál Fried

Arnold Friedman

Othon Friesz $1,000,000

Terry Frost

Ludovít Fulla

Eugène Gabritschevsky

James Gahagan

Vasudeo S. Gaitonde

Michael B. Gallagher

Glenn Gant

Pablo Gargallo

Louis-Edouard Garrido

Lee Gatch

William Gear

Angela Gegg

Annick Gendron

Ivan Generalic

Herbert Gentry

Abdullah Gërguri

Antonia Gerstacker

Mark Gertler

Gunther Gerszo

Leo Gestel

Araceli Gilbert

Stephen Gilbert

Sam Gilliam

William Glackens

Oton Gliha

Hermann Glöckner

Go Hui-dong

Alain Godon

Michael Goldberg

Peter Golfinopoulos

Salvador Gonzáles Escalona

Julio González

Catherine Goodman

Robert Goodnough

Leo Götz

Allan Graham

Gloria Graham

John D. Graham

Eugenio Granell

Nicolas Granger-Taylor

Cleve Gray

Reginald Gray

Balcomb Greene

Michail Grobman

Marcel Gromaire

George Grosz $150,000

Isaac Grünewald

Grupo Antillano

Frank Guild

Guilloume

Ismail Gulgee

Ella Guru

James Guthrie

Judith Gutiérrez

Ernst Haider

Fred S. Haines

Stacha Halpern

Elaine Hamilton-O'Neal

Pat Hanly

Murray Hantman

David Hare

Marsden Hartley $1,652,500

Hans Hartung

Ervin Hatibi

Julius Hatofsky

Julian Hatton

Grant Hayunga

Clive Head

André Hébuterne

Jeanne Hébuterne

Al Held

Jean Hélion

Gottfried Helnwein

Patrick Hennessy

Mary Henry

Auguste Herbin

Rowland Hilder

Sigrid Hjertén

Heinrich Hoerle

Hans Hofmann $4,297,000

Edward Hopper $26,800,000

Ralph Hotere

Robert H. Hudson

Leslie Hunter

Peter Hurd

Jörg Immendorff

Robert Indiana $500,000

Cynthia Ona Innis

Robert Irwin

James Lawrence Isherwood

Marvin Israel

István Sándorfi

María Izquierdo

Abby Jackson

Max Jacob

Frederic James

Daniel du Janerand

Donald Jarvis

Ferenc Joachim

Viggo Johansen

George Johnson

Lois Mailou Jones

Barbara Jones

Asger Jorn $2,099,500

Leonel Jules

Frida Kahlo $5,616,000

Wolf Kahn

Galina Kakovkina

Canuto Kallan

Kanda Nissho

Wassily Kandinsky $40,000,000

Rajmund Kanelba

Nabil Kanso

Stanislawa de Karlowska

David Kassan

Aart Kemink

Earl Kerkam

Maude Kerns

Daniel Patrick Kessler

Gayane Khachaturian

Michel Kikoine

Richard Killeen

Anna King

Eduardo Kingman

Ernst Ludwig Kirchner

Per Kirkeby

Moise Kisling

Jóhannes Sveinsson Kjarval

Cesar Klein

Joseph Kleitsch

Erika Giovanna Klien

Franz Kline $6,400,000

Georg Klusemann

Yasuhide Kobashi

Shalom Koboshvili

Ibrahim Kodra

Kiki Kogelnik

Helmut Kolle

Käthe Kollwitz $299,000

Darell Koons

Gojmir Anton Kos

Albert Kotin

Pinchus Kremegne

Irving Kriesberg

Nicholas Krushenick

Lev Kublanov

Robert Kulicke

Wifredo Lam

Mark Lammert

Ronnie Landfield

André Lanskoy

François Lanzi

Jacques Henri Lartigue

Maria Lassnig

Marie Laurencin $1,300,000

Frederick William Lawrence

Ernest Lawson

T. Allen Lawson

Louis le Brocquy

Bart van der Leck

Fernand Leduc

Luc Leestemaker

Fernand Léger $2,422,500

Felix Lembersky

Jean Paul Lemieux

Robert Lenkiewicz

Frances Lennon

Pavel Leonov

Levchenko Yaroslav

Hayley Lever

Rudolf Levy

Bill Lewis

Clayton Lewis

Norman Lewis

Loren Ligorio

Guy Lipscomb

Esteban Lisa

Carl Locher

Michael Loew

German Londoño

Will Longstaff

Morris Louis

L. S. Lowry

George Luks

Lunara

Jean Lurçat

Joseph Henry Lynch

Peter McArdle

Robert MacBryde

Colin McCahon

Mandy McCartin

John W. McCoy

Thoreau MacDonald

Stanton Macdonald-Wright (Van Vranken) $2,200,000

António Macedo

Henry Lee McFee

Edward McGuire

Palo Macho

Pete McKee

Iain Macnab

John McNamara

Karl Madsen

René Magritte $12,700,000

Estuardo Maldonado

Kazimir Malevich $17,000,000

Georges Malkine

Maruja Mallo

Mahirwan Mamtani

Sylvia Plimack Mangold

Edward Middleton Manigault

Franz Marc $5,061,500

Conrad Marca-Relli

Adam Marczynski

Albert Marquet

John de Martelly

Agnes Martin

Knox Martin

Ezio Martinelli

Alberto Martini

Ferenc Martyn

Guido Marzulli

Frans Masereel

Judith Mason

André Masson $400,000

Harry Mathes

Henri Matisse $18,496,000

Louisa Matthíasdóttir

Jan Matulka

Mike Mayhew

Mechtilt

Roger Medearis

Mikuláš Medek

Bouktje Medema

Vadym Meller

Haley Mellin

Milton Menasco

Theodore Mendez

Bernard Meninsky

Carlo Mense

Saülo Mercader

Richard Merkin

Marshall Merritt

Ralf Metzenmacher

Jean Metzinger $700.000

Jan Meyer

Peter Michael

Eduardo Michaelsen

Henri Michaux

Willard Midgette

Vasa Mihich

Mikey Georgeson

Ivan Milev

Manolo Millares

Oleg Minko

Sofia Minson

Luis Miranda

Joan Miró

Luna H. Mitani

Dean Mitchell

Fred Mitchell

Joan Mitchell $9,300,000

Albert Pinkham Ryder

Amedeo Modigliani $31,300,000

László Moholy-Nagy $5000

Alexander Mohr

Guido Molinari

Luis Molinari

Piet Mondrian $40,000,000

Paul Monnier

Giorgio Morandi

Teodor Moraru

Camilo Mori

Maritza Morillas

Hiroyuki Moriyama

Marcel Mouly

Jean-Paul Mousseau

Otto Muehl

Stephen Mueller

Jan Müller

Charles Munch

Loren Munk

Gerald and Sara Murphy

Peter Murphy

Archie Musick

Jonathan Myles-Lea

Abdul Rahim Nagori

Juan de los Angeles Naranjo

John Nash

Jørgen Nash

Paul Nash

Robert Natkin

Eva Navarro

Radi Nedelchev

Riitta Nelimarkka

Ismael Nery

Jackson Lee Nesbitt

Christopher R. W. Nevinson

Barnett Newman

Alexander Ney

Ben Nicholson

Jo Niemeyer

Nikos Nikolaou

Solomon Nikritin

Kenneth Noland

Emil Nolde $1,500,000

Vladimír Novák

Felix Nussbaum

Alejandro Obregón

Bencho Obreshkov

Hughie O'Donoghue

Juan O'Gorman

Georgia O'Keeffe $6,166,000

Jules Olitski

Robert Olley

Gaston Orellana

Manuel Ortiz de Zárate

Erik Ortvad

Piet Ouborg

Wolfgang Paalen

Natalia Pankova

Stass Paraskos

David Park

Ray Parker

Jürgen Partenheimer

Celia Paul

Gen Paul

Dave Pearson

Max Pechstein $1,400,740

Margot Peet

Waldo Peirce

Lucia Peka

Alfred Pellan

Jacques Pellegrin

Vincent Pepi

Samuel Peploe

Guilloume Perez-Zapata

Kuzma Petrov-Vodkin

Nadežda Petrovic

Tom Phillips

Francis Picabia $4,780,880

Pablo Picasso $106,500,000

John Piper

Armando Pizzinato

Angel Planells

Larry Poons

Fairfield Porter

Candido Portinari

Richard Pousette-Dart

Harold Septimus Power

Augusta Preitinger

David R. Prentice

Gregorio Prestopino

Alice Prin

Paine Proffitt

Hans Purrmann

Peter Purves Smith

José Puyet

Benito Quinquela Martín

Robert Raack

Anton Räderscheidt

Arnulf Rainer

Robert E. L. Rainey

Joseph Raphael

Sarah Raphael

Robert Rauschenberg $7,260,000

Isabel Rawsthorne

Mirko Racki

Hilla von Rebay

Willy Reetz

Paula Rego

Jack Reilly

Ad Reinhardt

Siegfried Reinhardt

Deborah Remington

Manuel Rendón Seminario

Paul Resika

Osvaldo Reyes

Carola Richards

RifRaf

Bridget Riley

Jean-Paul Riopelle

Will Roberts

Frederick Cayley Robinson

Keith Rocco

Danièle Rochon

William Ronald

Guy Rose

Mike Rose

Gaëtan de Rosnay

Gale Fulton Ross

Pierre Roy

Endre Rozsda

Nadya Rusheva

Morgan Russell

Luigi Russolo $420,000

Tomasz Rut

Anne Ryan

Alexander Sachal

Yuzo Saeki

Sanejouand

Raul Santoserpa

B. C. Sanyal

Sanyu

Giulio Aristide Sartorio

Aligi Sassu

Antonio Saura

Anne Savage

Jenny Saville

Bentley Schaad

Christian Schad

Martina Schettina

Eduardo Schlageter

Rudolf Schlichter

Hans-Jürgen Schlieker

Karl Schmidt-Rottluff

Jon Schueler

William S. Schwartz

John Seery

Simon Segal

Franz Wilhelm Seiwert

Andre Seleanu

Charles Seliger

Eusebio Sempere

Sueo Serisawa

Georges Seurat $35,200,000

Bettina Shaw-Lawrence

Robert B. Sherman

Lee Shi-min

Henrietta Shore

Harry Shoulberg

Jorge L. Sicre-Gattorno

Nora Simpson

Alfredo Sinclair

Mario Sironi $450,000

Sonya Sklaroff

John French Sloan

Hughie Lee-Smith

Jori Smith

Collier Twentyman Smithers

Koloman Sokol

William Sommer

Chaim Soutine

Amadeo de Souza Cardoso

Stanley Spencer $2,307,690

Sebastian Spreng

Steven Spurrier

Nicolas de Staël

Theodoros Stamos

Julian Stanczak

Joe Stefanelli

Zamy Steynovitz

Ary Stillman

Edgar Stoëbel

Thelma Johnson Streat

Aurelio Suárez

Alberto Sughi

Altoon Sultan

Francesca Sundsten

Léopold Survage

Graham Sutherland

Svavar Guðnason

Patrick Swift

Zdenek Sýkora

Stefan Szczesny

Marek Szwarc

Fernando de Szyszlo

Enrique Tábara

Massimo Taccon

Pierre Tal-Coat

Regan Tamanui

Rufino Tamayo

Yves Tanguy $2,250,000

Henry Ossawa Tanner

Antoni Tàpies

Verner Thomé

Edward H. Thompson

Sydney Lough Thompson

Harry Thubron

Jean Tirilly

Mark Tobey

Bradley Walker Tomlin $150,000

Charley Toorop

Rubén Torres Llorca

Carlos Trillo Name

Michel Trinquier

Don Troiani

Magdalena Trzebiatowska

Tsai Yulong

John Tunnard

William Ralph Turner

Laurits Tuxen

Cy Twombly

Nadezhda Udaltsova

Alan Uglow

Euan Uglow

Masumi Uno

Carlos Rafael Uribazo Garrido

Windsor Utley

Maurice Utrillo

Fausto Vagnetti

Sandor Vago

Suzanne Valadon

Maksimilijan Vanka

Victor Vasarely

Marie Vassilieff

Lydia Venieri

Lesbia Vent Dumois

James Verbicky

Verika

Paule Vézelay

Frederick Vezin

Esteban Vicente

Robert Vickrey

Hilda Vidal Valdés

Maria Helena Vieira da Silva

Jesús Carles de Vilallonga

Aníbal Villacís

Juan Villafuerte

Oscar Villalón

Oswaldo Viteri

Heinrich Vogeler

Ernst Rudolf Vogenauer

Richard Von White

Marie Vorobieff

John Henry Waddell

Edouard Wah

Lucille Wallenrod

Gordon Walters

Wang Yan Cheng

Vernon Ward

James W. Washington, Jr.

Max Weber

Shraga Weil

Jerry Weiss

Neil Welliver

Edward Wesson

Harold Weston

Rex Whistler

Neil Williams

William T. Williams

Jeff Willmore

Andrew Winter

Stanislaw Ignacy Witkiewicz

Emerson Woelffer

Wols

Paul Wonner

Christopher Wood

Joash Woodrow

Richard Caton Woodville

Troels Wörsel

Leon Wyczólkowski

Andrew Wyeth

Carolyn Wyeth

Constantin Xenakis

Xul Solar

Abraham Yakin

Taro Yamamoto

Yitzhak Yamin

Yao Youxin

Levchenko Yaroslav

Fred Yates

Manoucher Yektai

Peter Young

Marlene Tseng Yu

Adja Yunkers

Lisa Yuskavage

Jean-Pierre Yvaral

Mearson Daniel Zafra Pérez

Karl Zerbe

Ernest Zobole

Marguerite Zorach

Larry Zox

Jan Zrzavý

1880 - 1920s Post Impressionism Artists
Paul Cezanne $60,500,000

Vincent Van Gogh $82,500,000

Paul Gauguin $40,330,000

Georges Seurat $35,200,000

Henri-Edmund Cross

Maurice Prendergast

1880 - 1890 Art Nouveau Artists
Gustav Klimt $135,000,000

Aubrey Beardsley $49,000

Alphonse Mucha $100,000

Egon Schiele $23,287,850

Henri de Toulouse-Lautrec $22,416,000

1890s - 1920s Expressionism Artists

Francisco de Goya

Vincent van Gogh $82,500,000

Albert Pinkham Ryder

Edvard Munch $7,000,000

Georges Roualt $1,760,000

Egon Schiele $23,287,850

Franz Marc $5,061,500

August Macke $3,810,040

Lovis Corinth

Max Beckmann $3,200,000

Ernst Ludwig Kirchner

Alexei Jawlensky $8,296,000

Oskar Kokoschka $2,700,000

Emil Nolde $1,500,000

Jean Dubuffet $5,000,000

Francis Bacon $27,598,000

Lucian Freud $33,600,000

1903 - 1907 Fauvism Artists

Henri Matisse 1869-1954 $18,496,000

Louis Valtat 1869-1952

Georges Rouault 1871-1958 $1,760,000

Henri Manguin 1874-1949

Albert Marquet 1875-1947

Jean Puy 1876-1960

Maurice de Vlaminck

1876-1958 $10,721,805

Kees van Dongen 1877-1968

Raoul Dufy 1877-1953 $6,000,000

Charles Camoin 1879-1965

Othon Friesz 1879-1949 $1,000,000

Andre Derain 1880-1954 $6,848,000

Georges Braque 1882-1963 $8,640,000

Ben Benn 1884-1983

Roger de la Fresnaye 1885-1925

Marguerite Thompson Zorach 1887-1968

1905 -1939 Cubism Artists

Lyonel Feininger 1871-1956 $7,688,888

Jacques Villon 1875-1963

Raymond Duchamp-Villon 1876-1918 $1,762,500

Kasimir Malevich 1878-1935 $17,000,000

Maria Blanchard 1881-1932

Patrick Henry Bruce 1881-1936 $1,215,750

Albert Gleizes 1881-1953

Natalia Goncharova 1881-1962 $10,870,500

Fernand Leger 1881-1955 $22,407,500

Mikhail Larionov 1881-1964 $3,200,000

Henri Le Fauconnier 1881-1946 $45,000

Pablo Picasso 1881-1973 $106,500,000

Georges Braque 1882-1963 $8,640,000

Louis Marcoussis 1883-1941 $385,000

Jean Metzinger 1883-1956 $700.000

Gino Severini 1883-1966 $3,300,000

Robert Delaunay 1885-1941 $5,170,000

Roger de la Fresnaye 1885-1925

Henri Laurens 1885-1954 $1,472,000

Andre Lhote 1885-1962

Alexander Archipenko 1887-1964 $2,667,408

Juan Gris 1887-1927 $8,479,500

Henri Gaudier-Brzeska 1891-1915

Jacques Lipchitz 1891-1973

1916 -1922 Dada and 1924 - 1930s
Surrealism Artists

Hieronymous Bosch

Giorgio de Chirico

Jean Arp

Balthus

Marc Chagall $13,500,000

Joseph Cornell $400,000

Salvador Dali $4,126,680

Marcel Duchamp $1,762,500

Max Ernst $2,429,500

Alberto Giacometti $103,900,000

Raoul Hausmann

Frida Kahlo

Rene Magritte $12,700,000

Man Ray $1,504,440

Joan Miro $12,600,000

Kurt Schwitters $170,000

1920s - 1940s Bauhaus Artists

Walter Gropius $1300

Ludwig Mies van der Rohe

Lyonel Feininger $7,688,888

Paul Klee $7,000,000

Wassily Kandinsky $40,000,000

Oskar Schlemmer $420,000

Laszlo Moholy-Nagy $5000

Johannes Itten $25,000

Josef Albers $1,136,000

Anni Albers.

Gunta Stolzl

Lux Feininger

Wilhelm Wagenfeld

George Grosz $150,000

1909 - 1917 Futurism Artists

Umberto Boccioni $600,000

Giacomo Balla $4,400,000

Franz Marc $5,061,500

Kandinsky $40,000,000

Franco T. Marinetti $15,000

1920s - 1940's Harlem Renaissance

William H. Johnson $40,000

Lois Mailou Jones $14,000

Sargent Claude Johnson $1000

Jacob Lawrence $65,000

Archibald Motley $1000

Romare Bearden $70,000

Charles Sebree $12,000

Hale Woodruff $8000

Beauford Delaney $24,000

John Biggers $1000

Ernie Barnes $1000

1920's - 1940's Charleston Renaissance Artists

Elizabeth O'Neill Verner $15,000

Alfred Heber Hutty $5000

Alice Ravenel Huger Smith $6000

Corrie McCallum $1350

Independents (Oporto artist group) 1943 -1950
Abstract Art linked to the Portuguese Independents
Exhibitions, started by the artist Fernando Lanhas.

Nadir Afonso

Aníbal Alcino

António Azevedo

Sousa Caldas

Manuel da Cunha Monteiro

M. Félix de Brito

Dordio Gomes

Maria Graciosa de Carvalho

Carlos João Chambers Ramos

Fernando Lanhas

António Lino

Altino Maia

Joaquim Meireles

Henrique Moreira

Vítor Palla

Manuel Pereira da Silva

Rui Pimentel

Júlio Pomar

Júlio Resende

Arlindo Rocha

Abel Salazar

Amândio Silva

Augusto Tavares

Eduardo Tavares

Serafim Teixeira

Mário Truta

1945 - Present Abstract Expressionism Artists

Milton Avery

Willem De Kooning $63,500,000

Helen Frankenthaler $800,000

Philip Guston $1,183,500

Franz Kline $6,400,000

Joan Mitchell $9,300,000

Jackson Pollock $140,000,000

Mark Rothko $3,000,000

Cy Twombly

1950s/60s Op Art

Victor Vasarely

Josef Albers $1,136,000

M.C. Escher

Bridget Riley

Richard Anuszkiewicz

François Morellet

Jesús-Rafael Soto

1960s - Present Pop Art Artists

Jasper Johns $80,000,000

Robert Rauschenberg $7,260,000

Andy Warhol $71,700,000

Roy Lichtenstein

David Hockney $5,407,407

R. B. Kitaj $3,000,000

Keith Haring

Sigmar Polke

1970s - Present Minimalism

Andy Warhol $71,700,000

Jean-Michel Basquiat $5,509,500

Joseph Beuys

Anselm Kiefer

Sigmar Polke

Jeorg Immendorff

Gerhard Richter $20,800,000

Markus Luepertz

Howard Hodgkin

Ed Kienholz

Cy Twombly

Philip Pearlstein

Eric Fischl

Mark Tansey

Keith Haring

Francesco Clemente

Sidney Goodman

Damien Hirst

Some Other great Art Reference and Art Dealer Magazines you should be on the lookout for

20x20 magazine

Aesthetica - The Art

and Culture Magazine

American Art Review

Aperture

Apollo - monthly

Art and Antiques

Art and Architecture Journal

Art+Auction

Art & Project

The Artist's Magazine

Artforum

Artnet

Artibus Asiae

Artist Profile

Artibus et Historiae

Art in America est. 1913

ARTINFO

ArtAsiaPacific

Art of England

Art on paper -

Art Monthly

The Art Newspaper

ART PAPERS

ARTnews - founded in 1902

ArtPulse

ArtReview - est. London, 1949

Art Signature File, G.B. David

Arts Magazine published 1926–1992

Atlantica Revista de Arte y

Pensamiento, Centro Atlántico

de Arte de Moderno (CAAM)

Australian Art Collector

Australian Art Review

Bedeutung

Blueprint

The Blue Review published in 1913

BAK magazine,

The Bear Deluxe

BOMB Magazine

The Brooklyn Rail

The Burlington Magazine est. 1903

Constance

Contemporary

Contemporary Art Philippines

Corridor8

Culture Lounge

KIOSK

CUSS

Daruma Magazine

Dialogue

Die Insel - 1899-1901

The Drama

Esopus

Fillip

Flash Art

Fotoblur

frieze

Hunter and Cook

ImagineFX

The Jackdaw

Lens Culture

McJAWN

Metronome

Minotaure - (1933-1939)

Miriskusstva - est. 1899
in St. Petersburg, Russia

Modern Painters

Moving Art Magazine

New Art Examiner

n.paradoxa

NYArts

Parkett

The Pastel Journal

Photosho

PLAZM

Portfolio Magazine

Print Connoisseur - 1920 - 1932

Raw Vision

Revolutionart -

Revue Noire, Paris, 1991-2001.

Sculpture

Sensitive Skin Magazine

Triple Canopy (online magazine)

The Art Signature File, G.B. David

Third Text

TradeArt

Wallpaper

Watercolor Artist

White Fungus Magazine

Whitehot Magazine

of Contemporary Art

X, London, 1959-62

Zingmagazine

Some Examples of antique frame auction sales records

American, 1937 Carved, polychromed, and gilded By Walfred Thulin, signed and dated on verso Opening size: 33 1/2" x 30 3/8" Molding width: 3" Original period frame price $45,000

American, c. 1930 Carved and silver leafed three step molding Opening size: 13 5/8" x 9 3/8" Molding width: 2" Original period frame price $9,500

American, c. 1920 Applied ornament and gilded Opening size: 28 1/2" x 26" Molding width: 6" Original period frame price $35,000

American, c. 1920's Carved and gilded By Robert Laurent, signed on verso Opening size: 19 1/2" x 15 5/8" Molding width: 2 3/8" Original period frame price $30,000

American, c. 1920 Carved and gilded By Copley Gallery, Boston, medallion on verso Opening size: 25 3/8" x 19 1/4" Molding width: 3 5/8" Original period frame price $24,000

American, c. 1920 Carved, gilded and painted By Bernard Badura, New Hope, PA, signed on Verso Opening size: 23 3/8" x 19 1/2" Molding width: 2 7/8" Original period frame price $26,000

American, c. 1920's Carved and gilded By Robert Laurent, signed on verso Opening size: 23 3/8" x 17 5/8" Molding width: 4 5/8" Original period frame price $35,000

American, c. 1920 Carved, gilded, painted and incised By Max Kuehne Opening size: 31 1/8" x 23" Molding width: 3 1/2" Original period frame price $65,000

Places art dealers buy, sell and auction art

Artstar.com USA

Biddington's - USA online auction

Ewolfs.com - USA

Nickleby's International Auctions - USA

Auktionshaus Zeller - Lindau, Germany

ExtraLot - Germany

Hildener Auktionshaus Dahmann

Hilden /Duesseldorf, Germany

Hans-Dieter Dahmann

Print World - Munich, Germany

Ukiyo-e World - Pullach, Germany

Auction by ADEC - Paris, France

Etude Aguttes

Neuilly-sur-Seine, France

Etude Cornette de Saint Cyr

Paris, France[live]

Etude Mercier - Lille, France[live]

The Etude MERCIER & Cie

Etude Millon & AssociTs - Paris, France

Etude NTret-Minet - Paris, France

Nart - France & online]

PIASA - Paris,

France French auctioneers

Artconte - Contemporary art auction –

London, United Kingdom

ArtLondon.Com - United Kingdom

Bonhams - London, United Kingdom

Christie's - London, United Kingdom

London Art Auctions –

London, United Kingdom

Phillips International Auctioneers

London, United Kingdom

The Auction Channel - London

Ha.com - Ha.com

ShopGoodWill

Liveauctioneers.com

Icollector.com

Hakes.com

SoldUSA.com

Ubid.com

Delcampe

Bonanzle.com

Goantiques.com

Ecrater.com

Amazon.com

Blujay.com

Etsy.com

Atomicmall.com

Ioffer.com

Tias.com

Craigslist.org

Oodle.com

Apps.facebook.com/marketplace

Sell.com

Kijiji.com

eBid.net Collectible Auction

Old and Sold

OnlineAuction.com Collectible Auction

WeBidz Collectible Auctions

Webstore Collectible Auctions

UpperBid Collectibles

Cqout.com

Collectibles.bidstart.com

Epier.com

Auctions at ePier.com

Playle.com

Auctionfire.com

Sothebys.com

Fineart.ha.com

Christies.com

Bonhams & Butterfield

Liveauctioneers.com

iCollector.com

Artnet.com

iGavel

Coeur D'Alene Art

Los Angeles Modern Art Auctions

Phillips de Pury & Co.

Swann Galleries

Doyle New York

Saffronart

Art Fortune

Leslie Hindman Auctioneers

140Hours

Shannon's Fine Art Auctioneers

Israeli Art Auction

Baterbys Art Auction Gallery

Gray's Auctioneers & Appraisers

Aspire Auctions

Cowan Auctions

Sante Fe Art Auction

Slotin Folk Art

Rago Arts

Freeman's

Scottsdale Art Auction

MassArt Benefit Auction

Art Papers

Dallas Auction Gallery

Shopgoodwill.com

Propertyroom.com

Policeauctions.com

Seizedpropertyauctions.com

eBid.net

CQout.com

Artbyus.com

Onlineauction.com

Webstore.com

WeBidz.com

upperbid.com

Aantv.com

Amazon.com

Etsy.com

Delcampe.net

Bonanzle.com

Ecrater.com -

Goantiques.com

Art.rubylane.com

Blujay.com

Atomicmall.com

iOffer.com

Tias.com

Craigslist.org

Oodle.com

Sell.com

Kijiji.com

Special Art Dealer Research Libraries

One of the best reference sources for art research is the Thomas J. Watson Library which has access to the below listed resources

http://libmma.org/portal/e-resources/

AAT: Art & Architecture Thesaurus Online (Getty Research Institute)

ACLS Humanities E-Book

Allgemeines Künstlerlexikon (World Biographical Dictionary of Artists)

American National Biography Online (ANB)

American Periodical Series Online

Ancestry Library Edition

Archives Directory for the History of Collecting in America

Art Sales Catalogues online (ACS) (1600 – 1900)

Art Sales Index (1970 – present)

Art Theorists of the Italian Renaissance

ArtFact Pro (1986 – present)

ArtNet (1985 – present)

AskART

Benezit Dictionary of Artists

Berg Fashion Library

Britannica Online

CAMEO (Conservation and Art
Material Encyclopedia Online)

China Academic Journals (CAJ
full-text database: Series F,
Literature, history, philosophy)

Columbia Gazetteer of the World

Dictionary of Art Historians

Dictionary of National Biography

Early American Newspapers, Series 1-3, 1690 -1922

Encyclopaedia of Islam

Europa Sacra

Getty Provenance Index

Getty Thesaurus of Geographic
Names Online

Gordon's Photography Prices (1970 – present)

Gordon's Print Price Annual (1986 – present)

Grove Art Online

Grove Music Online

HeritageQuest Online

Historical Clippings Finding
Aid (1880 – 1980)

Humanities E-Book

JAANUS

Lexikon des Mittelalters online

Lugt's Répertoire online (1600 – 1900)

Marquis Who's Who on the Web

Mayer Auction Records

New York Times Historical Newspapers
from ProQuest (1851 – 2007)

Oxford Art Online

Oxford Language Dictionaries
Online (OLDO)

Oxford Reference Online Premium

Reallexikon zur Deutschen
Kunstgeschichte

Rhizome.org and Rhizome ArtBase

RKD Databases

SCIPIO: Art and Rare Book
Sales Catalogs

The Chicago Manual of Style Online

The Nazi-Era Provenance
Internet Portal Project

The Times Digital Archive (1785 – 1985)

Timeline of Art History

ULAN: Union List of
Artist Names Online

WBIS (World Biographical
Information System)

Webster's Third New
International Dictionary Unabridged

Who's Who in American Art

Who's Who in American History

WorldCat / WorldCat.org

Libraries, Archives, and Study Centers of The

Metropolitan Museum of Art Libraries Open to Public, with

Request to the Collections

American Wing Library

Ancient Near East

Antonio Ratti Textile Center

Arms and Armor

Arts of Africa, Oceania, and

the Americas, Robert Goldwater

Library & Photograph Study Collection

Asian Art Library

Cloisters Library and Archives

Costume Institute,

Irene Lewisohn Costume Library

Departmental Libraries with

Requestable Collections

and/or Open by Appointment

Drawings and Prints, Reference

Collection and Study Rooms

Egyptian Art

European Paintings

European Sculpture and

Decorative Arts

Image Library

Islamic Art

Medieval Art

Modern Art Library

Museum Archives

Musical Instruments

Nolen Library

Objects Conservation

Painting Conservation

Paper Conservation

Photographs, Joyce F. Menschel

Photography Library & Study Room

Robert Lehman Collection Library

Scientific Research

Textile Conservation

The Onassis Library for Hellenic and Roman Art in the Department of Greek and Roman Art

OtherArt Libraries

Archives of American Art

Archives of American Art

Catalog (Smithsonian Institution)

Art Inventories (SIRIS)

Art Libraries Network: Florence

Munich - Rome

Bibliographie nationale française

Catalogues de la Bibliotheque
nationale de France

Columbia Libraries
Information Online [CLIO]

Die Deutsche Bibliothek

Direction des Musées de France. Catalogue collectif
des bibliothèques des musées

Getty Research Library,
IRIS Main Menu

Harvard OnLine Library
Information System [HOLLIS]

IRIS - Consortium of Art History and Humanities
Libraries in Florence

Libdex

Libweb: Library Servers via WWW

National Art Library at the Victoria & Albert Museum
Computer Catalogue
nationaux.

New York Public Library [CATNYP]

New York University [BobCat]

Online Library Catalogs in the NYC Area

Princeton University Library,
Main Catalog

Ryerson and Burnham Libraries Catalog

Smithsonian Institution Research
Information System

The British Library

The Frick Research Catalog
Online [FRESCO]

The Library of Congress Online Catalog

The Museum of Modern Art Library, Archives and Study
Centers Online Catalog

Vatican Library. (Biblioteca Apostolica Vaticana) Online
Catalog

Virtueller Katalog
Kunstgeschichte (VKK)

Yale University Library,
Orbis and Library Catalogs

Bibliography

ARTIST AND PUBLIC AND OTHER ESSAYS ON ART
SUBJECTS BY KENYON COX 1914,
by Charles Scribner's Sons

NOTES AND QUERIES: A MEDIUM OF
INTER-COMMUNICATION FOR LITERARY MEN,
ARTISTS, ANTIQUARIES, GENEALOGISTS,
ETC. VOL. IV.—No. 95. 1851.

OUR ARTIST IN CUBA, PERU, SPAIN AND ALGIERS.
LEAVES FROM THE SKETCH-BOOK OF A
TRAVELLER. 1864-1868. BY GEORGE W. CARLETON.

ARTISTS PAST AND PRESENT RANDOM STUDIES
BY ELISABETH LUTHER CARY 1909

GREAT ARTISTS RAPHAEL RUBENS MURILLO
 DURER BY JENNIE ELLIS KEYSOR 1899

LIVES OF THE MOST EMINENT PAINTERS
SCULPTORS & ARCHITECTS
BY GIORGIO VASARI: BASTIANO TO TADDEO
ZUCCHERO 1914

THE COMPLETE WORKS OF JOHN RUSKIN
MODERN PAINTERS 1856

WOOD-BLOCK PRINTING A DESCRIPTION OF THE
CRAFT OF WOODCUTTING & COLOUR PRINTING
 BASED ON THE JAPANESE PRACTICE BY F.
MORLEY FLETCHER 1916

LIVES OF THE MOST EMINENT PAINTERS
SCULPTORS & ARCHITECTS
BY GIORGIO VASARI: TRIBOLO TO IL SODOMA
1914

ANECDOTES OF PAINTERS, ENGRAVERS Sculptors
and Architects, AND CURIOSITIES OF ART. BY S.
SPOONER, M. D., NEW YORK: 1853.

ART BY CLIVE BELL 1913

LIVES OF THE MOST EMINENT PAINTERS
SCULPTORS & ARCHITECTS
BY GIORGIO VASARI: VOLUME III. FILARETE AND
SIMONE TO MANTEGNA 1912

A HISTORY OF ART FOR BEGINNERS AND
STUDENTS PAINTING—SCULPTURE—

ARCHITECTURE BY CLARA ERSKINE CLEMENT 1887

LIVES OF THE MOST EMINENT PAINTERS SCULPTORS & ARCHITECTS BY GIORGIO VASARI: VOLUME VI. FRA GIOCONDO NICCOLÒ SOGGI 1913

CHINESE PAINTERS A CRITICAL STUDY BY RAPHAEL PETRUCCI 1920

LIVES OF THE MOST EMINENT PAINTERS SCULPTORS & ARCHITECTS 1912 By GIORGIO VASARI: THE FRENCH IMPRESSIONISTS (1860-1900) BY CAMILLE MAUCLAIR 1903

A TEXT-BOOK OF THE HISTORY OF PAINTING BY JOHN C. VAN DYKE, L.H.D. 1909 ANCIENT AND MEDIEVAL ART: A Short History By BULLEY, MARGARET Methuen, London, 1919. 2nd UK Edition

THE TABLE BOOK OF ART (1878) History of Art in all Countries and Ages By Sandhurst, P. T

THE MASTERPIECES OF FRENCH ART A BIOGRAPHICAL HISTORY OF ART IN FRANCE, FROM THE EARLIEST PERIOD TO AND INCLUDING THE SALON OF 1882 (VOLS. 1 & 2) Edited by William A. Armstrong By Viardot, Louis Encyclopedia America. A Popular Dictionary of Arts, Sciences, Literature, History, Politics and Biography including A copious Collection of Original Articles in American Biography on the Basis of the Seventh Edition of the German Author: edited by Francis Lieber assisted by E. Wigglesworth and T. G. Bradford 1829-1833

A Complete Dictionary of the Greek and Roman Antiquities, explaining the obscure places in classic authors, and ancient historians, relating to the religion, mythology, history, geography and chronology of the ancient Greeks and Romans; their sacred and profane rites and customs; laws, polity, arts and engines of war; also an account of their navigations, arts and sciences, and the inventors of them; with the lives and opinions of their philosophers
By DANET, Pierre (ca. 1650-1709)

Japan and China. Its History, Arts and Literature
By BRINKLEY, CAPTAIN F
London: T.C. & E.C. Jack, 1903

Les Clouet: Peintres officiels des Rois de France

[ART HISTORY, FRANCE]

By Moreau-Nelaton, Etienne Paris: 1908: Emile Levy.

Le Peintre-Graveur Francais, Catalogue Raisonne Des Estampes Gravees Par Les Peintres Et Les Dessinateurs De L'Ecole Francaise - by Robert-Dumesnil, A. P. F. & Baudicour, Prosper De 1835-1871

HAND-BOOK FOR TRAVELLERS IN SPAIN, AND READERS AT HOME. By Ford, Richard; John Murray London: John Murray., 1845.

The Islamic Book: A Contribution to Its Art and History from the VII-XVIII Century By Arnold, Thomas W.; Adolf Grohmann Pegasus Press. 1929

The Drawings of The Florentine Painters. Classified, Criticised and Studied as Documents In The History and Appreciation of Tuscan Art, with a Copious Catalogue Raisonne By Berenson, Bernhard London: John Murray. 1903.

Typographical Antiquities. History, Origin, and Progress, of the Art of Printing, from its First Invention...By LEMOINE, Henry London: S. Fisher, 1797

The Masterpieces of French Art Illustrated. by Viardot, Louis et al; Edited By Wm. A. Armstrong Philadelphia, PA: Gebbie & Co. Publishers 1885

Sculptura-historico-technica: or The history and art of ingraving London: Printed for S. Harding, on the Pavement in St. Martin's-Lane, 1747

HANDWRITTEN MANUSCRIPT STUDY OF FLORENTINE HISTORY AND ITALIAN ART 1907-1908 By RUTH ABBOTT ITALY, FLORENCE, NAPLES, 1908

PANTOLOGIA. A New Cyclopaedia... Alphabetically Arranged; with a General Dictionary of Arts, Sciences, and Words... By Good, John Mason and Olinthus Gregory and Newton Bosworth London: Printed for G. Kearsley et al.. 1813

Japan (and China). Its History Arts and Literature. Illustrated. By Brinkley, Captain F Boston and Tokyo: J. B. Millet Company, 1901

History of the Japanese Arts By Imperial Museum 1908. 2. Tokyo Teishitsu Hakubutsukan.

ENCYCLOPEDIA AMERICANA. A Popular Dictionary of Arts, Sciences, Literature, History, Politics and Biography...

Including... American Biography; on the Basis of the Seventh Edition of the German Conversations-Lexicons. Edited by Francis Lieber, Assisted by E. Wigglesworth [and T. G. Bradford]

By Lieber, Francis Philadelphia: Carey, Lea & Carey.. 1829-1833

Le Peintre-Graveur Francais, Catalogue Raisonne Des Estampes Gravees Par Les Peintres Et Les Dessinateurs De L'Ecole Francaise by P,, A,

The Masterpieces of French Art Illustrated, Being a Biographical History of Art in France, from the Earliest Period to and Including the Salon of 1882

By Louis Viardot and Other Writers

About the Author

David Valin is a Weekend Part Time Art Dealer in New York City. The author has been a successful art dealer for 35 years, in New York City, Boston and around the world. His successes have been a part of discovering, marketing and placing many a work of art for future generations to be able to view, learn and wonder about. He has journeyed through the back rooms of many museums, auction houses and galleries.

And has had the opportunity to research artworks on independent art research projects, in the Archives of American Art in Washington D.C., the Museum of Modern Art and many other fine reference libraries across the USA and overseas. In his travels he has met and befriended many part time and full time art dealers, and artists and benefited from the knowledge gained from their expertise in the rewarding field of art dealing.

www.ingramcontent.com/pod-product-compliance
Lightning Source LLC
Chambersburg PA
CBHW060236100426
42742CB00011B/1548